To God be the Glory! Fired from a teaching job I loved, the future looked dim. But then His gentle nudging brought forth the urge to write about my 46 years as a teacher. That God whisper lead to 19 months of recounting experiences of both frustration and joy.

Teachers are the greatest asset to this nation. Educators shape the future through the children they inspire. If you have a pulse, you have a purpose! Be the voice for today's teachers.

Rescue the Teacher, Save the Child!

Paula Baack

Baack to School Press—Monument, CO
ISBN: 978-0-578-48044-2
Library of Congress Control Number: 2019903318
Title: *Rescue the Teacher, Save the Child!*
Author: Paula Baack
Digital distribution | 2019
Paperback Edition | 2019
Edited by Christina Alexander

DEDICATION

This book is dedicated to Charles Bowling II who joined the angels in heaven too soon. He demonstrated, through his love of music, a black man and a white woman could share their cultures. Through collaboration, we accomplished this by teaching hundreds of students to perform. Our friendship spanned 35 years. Hopefully the impact of music on our students lasts a lifetime. When composing Brother Charles' eulogy, I discovered writing came easy when the subject matter consisted of a dear friend who loved being a teacher. After Charles was laid to rest, I felt God nudging me to record my accumulated stories regarding the lovely, albeit challenging experiences of teaching. I am certain Charles would have encouraged me. This is for you, my brother.

ABOUT THE AUTHOR

A teacher for 46 years in three states, 15 schools, 17 classrooms and 17 grade levels (Kindergarten through college), Paula Baack taught over 6000 children through adult singers; in addition she directed youth, collegiate and adult choral ensembles (public schools, university, community college and churches)

- Received regional and national recognition for her work in vocal studies
- Recognized as the 2017 Outstanding Director in Choral Education by the Colorado Springs Chorale
- Received recognition in 2015 for her work with Down Syndrome children
- Received the 2014 Boettcher Colorado Teacher Recognition Award
- In 2010, invited to present her paper "Assessing the Singer, Making the Choir Accountable" to the Third International Symposium on Assessment in Music Education held in Bremen, Germany
- Who's Who in Education 2007
- Master Teacher with Sedona Jazz on the Rocks, where Mrs. Baack was a featured artist with her vocal jazz group La Petite JaZaz (2005-2006)
- Who's Who of American Teachers (2000 & 2004)
- Several of Mrs. Baack's former students are performing or have performed on the national stage: Scottie Johnson with *Gin Blossoms*; Scott MacIntyre was Top 8 in Season 9 of *American Idol*; Todd MacIntyre performed on the national tour of *Mama Mia*; James Valentine is singer/guitarist with *Maroon 5*; Nate Zuercher performs with *Judah and the Lion*

FOREWORD

My name is Paula Baack. I am a recovering educator. Here are my
five steps*:

1. I admit I am powerless over my fate as an educator.
2. By God's Grace, I survived 46 years of teaching, loving it
   more each year.
3. The decision to turn over days of anxiety, frustration,
   physical depletion and mental deprivation to God, helped
   me stay the course.
4. I gave serious consideration and reflection to the many
   positions I held in the past. I embraced the embarrassing
   moments in front of the classroom and the guilt I felt by not
   spending more time with my family.
5. I admit to some errors in judgment, lack of empathy on
   occasion, and just being plain stubborn.

*Adapted from Alcoholics Anonymous

The names of students, colleagues, parents, institutions and
administrators have been changed to protect both the innocent and
the guilty. While the anecdotes hold truth, incidents and genders
altered to assure anonymity. The exceptions are: Vaughn Jaenike,
the head of music education at the University of Nebraska, Lincoln;
Ruth Jaenike, his wife, who was my cooperating teacher; Marva
Collins, who set the national standards high when working with at
risk children; Barbara Colorosa, who instilled positive teaching
practices.

TABLE OF CONTENTS

Chapter 12: New Voices, New Mountains

- Retirement Or Permanent Vacation?
- The 4:41 Forgiveness Plan
- Pursue Pause
- Two Cents Worth With Change Back
- The Legend Of The Horse
- Method To My Madness
- Andrea's Voice
- The Still Small Voice Within
- New Voices
- Making a Difference
- New Mountains

CHAPTER 1: A NOBLE PROFESSION

I am a Teacher: That is to say I was a teacher until I was summarily dismissed, fired, forced to retire on April 25, 2017. I am not sure which term fits my demise best.

On April 24, 2017, talented singers filled positions in all of our eight choirs. Several ensembles had competed successfully on the international, national, and state levels. Our choirs consistently gained yearly recognition by the state activities organization at their annual gala. February of 2017, we held auditions for the coming year and every choir filled with students who loved to perform. In March, I took a group of singers to tour New York City, see three Broadway shows, and participate in two clinics with Broadway actors. On April 24, 2017, it would be fair to say I was comfortable in my position and worked relentlessly to sustain that feeling.

On April 26, 2017, cowering at home, I felt light headed with heart palpitations. A pit formed in my stomach like none other experienced before. I felt hurt, confused and betrayed. My Christian belief system went to work. I prayed, but not the prayers of praise and thanksgiving. No prayer passed my lips thanking God for the privilege of being a teacher. All I could mutter was, "Why me, God? Really?" The day previous to this, my 46 years as a career teacher, came to an abrupt end.

April 25, 2017, I walked with confidence toward the administrative offices for my End of the Year (EOY) evaluation. I had undergone this process a number of times, so I felt no need to be nervous. For almost a decade, this teaching position held the expected challenges. My integrity and style of teaching underwent the usual questioning by my department and the administration. Not only had I survived, I thrived over the years and built a substantial program. While this year contained its usual ups and downs, why would this EOY be any different?

I am unable to bury the words I heard that day. "You will not be the choral director here next year. If you do chose to return, you will be placed where you cannot be a part of any negative student interaction and where you will have nothing to do with collecting money." My breath stopped. Swallowing hard, I tried to make sense of those words and started to ask questions. The voice raised in decibels, as if scolding a naughty child. "Did you not hear me? You are not going to be teaching choir here next year!"

My gravestone should read *She Never Saw It Coming*. In my personal life, many things shocked and blindsided me. As a defense mechanism, I crowned myself with a new title: *Queen of the Worst Case Scenarios*. I tried to foresee any negative event which could lead to my downfall and then attempted to navigate through it with composure. It seldom worked. April 25, 2017, was no different. I had not seen this coming.

As you take this journey alongside me, your points of view as a student, teacher, parent or administrator will shift as I encourage you to walk in one another's shoes. My story is laced with anecdotes of success, failure, passion and what it meant to be a teacher. April 25, 2017, was my day which will live in infamy. As dramatic as it may sound, this best describes the deepest hurt I ever experienced as a 46 year veteran teacher. But through God's grace, I am recovering.

Forty-six Years of Research: In high school, I knew two things would never occur in my collegiate study. I would not do anything in music and teaching kids was not in my wheelhouse. As a child, I rejected the idea of playing school. My parents required me to study piano, flute and organ.

Music became a forced playmate. She and I did not see eye to eye. Despite that, I found myself in the 1960's attending the state university studying organ and working towards a degree in music education. Having no life goals, I floated in any direction the wind blew. I spent my days serving as a student senator, skipping classes and partying. It was during the Viet Nam war, and many of us were not fixated on higher education. I drifted, lost. The head of the music department threatened to kick me out for missing classes. When I did attend, doing so half-heartedly, I muddled through. To this day, reoccurring nightmares plague me: I find myself attending school in a round building, where each floor rotates to a new position every hour. I cannot find my next classroom since the floor pivoted a half turn. I slide down sloping corridors, travel in elevators going sideways, and crawl through dark heating ducts in hopes of finding my class. During this nightmare, I run into classmates telling me I missed the final test. My sub conscience perceived university life as an absolute bad dream.

As it turned out, majoring in education became my lifeline. The department was headed by Dr. Vaughn Jaenike, whose leadership provided motivation for me. Student teaching saved my collegiate study from complete failure. Vaughn arranged my student teacher practicum with his wife, Ruth Jaenike. She met me in the hallway on my first day of student teaching as she was on her way out of the building to teach at another school. Hastily, Ruth informed me I would need to teach music to first graders on my own. How could I be expected to accomplish this on my first day? The teaching pedagogy received thus far had been minimal, so the concept of teaching by myself terrified me. To this day, I do not remember what I taught. But when the day came to an end, I adored teaching!

Ruth and I shared a collaborative spirit. We decided to approach music education through the humanities, encompassing singing, art, architecture, dance, theatre and symphonic music. Working with this incredible mentor produced the feelings of deep appreciation for the perfect job. At the end of each unit, we held culminating sessions with professionals from the community. Ruth lit the flame which began my passion to teach. I will always be thankful for Vaughn and Ruth's influence in my life.

But that flame sputtered. I was not ready to set the world on fire. My worst flaw was the inability to stay the course. Partying and sporadically attending classes did not provide a solid start in my first two years of college. When I decided to elope, the idea of settling down seemed reasonable. My last two years of undergraduate study were filled with perseverance to graduate with better grades. I finished my Bachelor of Science degree (majoring in both education and vocal performance) in 1971. My lucky break came when I received an offer to teach part time with Ruth. This allowed me to return to work on my Masters of Music degree at the same institution. I concentrated on becoming a professional singer. If I needed to put food on the table, I would use my teaching degree. I enjoyed another year with Ruth while completing my Masters. Having received my Master's degree in 1973 (both music education and vocal performance), becoming a career teacher was not my ambition. My limited vision plan involved getting hired as a full-time teacher, attaining tenure, quitting to have children. Then after our virtual children went to school, perhaps I would fall back on teaching.

The first year post Masters, I was hired to teach Kindergarten through second grade (K-2) general music in seven schools. It was an experiment where the theoretical benefits never actually manifested in the reality. That year my teammates and I changed schools every day at noon, directed 16 holiday programs and returned home exhausted at the end of each day. Teaching levels K-2, under those circumstances, never held the possibility of ever lighting a fire inside of me.

Next, I held a position as a full time general music teacher at an elementary school. The school contained no music room, so I traveled from classroom to classroom, wheeling a cart loaded with everything needed for the day. A small flame of passion began to glow brighter, but it would take a few years to ignite to a full burn. After my third year at this school, I resigned when I became pregnant (and tenured). I enjoyed the 18 months away from teaching and loving on our sweet little boy. During that period, I continued my voice studio, which afforded me an environment of instruction. But my aforementioned plan remained intact.

When my husband and I needed to supplement our income, I found a part time position at a lovely new school. The full-time music teacher and I hit it off immediately. She loved her job, and her talented students reflected her dedication. She and I designed units of study, which would include the entire school. Life was good.

Just when I started to relax in my role as wife, mother and teacher, the carpet was violently pulled out from underneath me. My husband of 10 years ended our marriage with the words "I no longer love you." My part-time position and voice studio helped me to survive, both financially and emotionally. As far as my aspirations for becoming a professional singer? They died with the reality of becoming a single parent.

Through that tumultuous time, I survived on knowing God watched over me and my son. After marrying my current husband, my first husband relinquished his parental rights. I will forever appreciate my former husband's final gesture.

God sends us special gifts along the way, which hold the power to divert us from the pain. My second marriage developed into decades of support from my husband, devoted to both me and our son. We celebrated our 38th wedding anniversary this past July.

Having worked part time for five years, I sought out a full time position. I was hired at an elementary school down the street. It prepared me for the reality when teaching could produce times of provocation. The environment was hostile and the music teacher viewed as being more support staff than part of the academic core. My final two years in elementary music education were spent there, having completed 12 years in all.

I felt positive I would never teach middle school (called junior high at that time; grades 7-9). Such psychotic kids! Whenever I would see a clump of them downtown, they ran through people, all the while screaming and laughing. Who could possibly want to teach those kids? I felt so assured of this truth that I never student taught at the junior high level. A junior high colleague phoned one day and asked if I would be interested in her job since she was leaving. I held no interest whatsoever. Not in the least bit discouraged, she argued how junior high would prove itself a great place for me. Then she said the magic words. I would receive two 50 minute planning periods per day. My mind reeled, stunned. At my present position, I had one and a half hours *per week* for planning. I taught 10-11 classes per day, back to back. I didn't care how wild those junior high kids acted. With 100 minutes per day of plan time, I could deal with any issues. So I opened a new book on my journey and welcomed a career as a music educator.

My junior high students never proved to reflect the rowdy kids I encountered at the mall. They were extremely gifted in vocal performance. The program grew from approximately 90 students to almost 500. In addition, the school hired another choral director to cover the large enrollment. Our choirs performed in the community 20-30 times per year. The successful turning point occurred early in my tenure when two incredibly talented young men joined the choir. They not only loved to sing, but their voices presented way beyond their years. Both showed tremendous athletic ability and were held in high esteem by their peers. Once they demonstrated guys singing as acceptable and common practice, our program never looked back. My principal enjoyed singing in choir throughout his high school career, so he supported our program wholeheartedly. The department was easy to work with and enjoyed spending social times together. While employed at that school those 15 years, my experience appeared a positive one. Now reflecting back, it was the best one of my career! My flame was not only lit, but the burning passion to provide students with the best music education experience became my new life goal. Music began to dance, playing her flute and swaying. I glanced at her, and the first glimmer of acceptance for my forced childhood friend began to form in my mind.

A choral position at the local university was epitomized as the end all job by many choral directors. The director, having started one the area's renowned show choirs, retired after 24 years. People from all over the region put their names in for the position, including me. My junior high students performed collegiate level music. I had dance experience as well, so I felt comfortable teaching choreography. Why couldn't a junior high teacher apply for the collegiate position? Even to my surprise, the directing nod came to me. Unfortunately this appointment was not one of the highlights of my career. I believe the students, influenced by my junior high teacher status, never thought me skilled enough. When this ensemble received an invitation to perform at Disney World as one of the top nine national collegiate groups, I thought the corner turned. But even with that success, no buy in existed from the students. Since the university position was part time, I continued teaching at the junior high and also directing the children's choir at a local church. Our only child went off to college, a good day's drive away. Filling the empty nest with "teaching on steroids" placed me on the edge of insanity. Something had to give, so I resigned all three of my positions. Those 27 years empowered me with so much confidence in my teaching ability. The joy of making music and a devoted work ethic generated a flame which would continue in my next destination. So my husband and I forged on to another state. Finally, I would retire, I thought.

Touted as a magical place, the Southwest held a certain magnetism. When we first moved there, picnics in December and wearing sandals year around had a definite appeal. I opened my voice studio, which proved productive. However, I missed the choral experience. After a few months I acquired a position at the local college to teach piano, voice class and private voice. The program grew as I added choirs to the department. I designed the vocal jazz curriculum for all 12 colleges in the state. The head of the choral department took a sabbatical and I was asked to take his place. I thought I reached the pinnacle of success. My pay bettered the professors at the local university, students came flocking to the program and I performed, for the first time, as a professional singer. It felt perfect. Or so I thought. The choral director, whom I replaced, decided to return. I became a thorn in his side as his program began competing with mine. So he did what any good administrator was prone to do. He took away my funding, in the hopes my program would go away. I gained fundraising knowledge early in my career, so this move became a minor deterrent. The students and I raised the money to support our performing groups.

Over those nine years, the state exploded in population. With all the new roadways, the asphalt absorbed the scorching sun, making everything unbearably hotter, longer. In addition, the performing arts department continually held high drama, so I decided to make a change. My husband and I missed the four seasons and the slower pace, so we moved up north. I would definitely retire now.

For the first two years in the land of snow and mountains, I thought my voice studio would fill my ache to teach music. It did for a while. But I longed for the chaos of directing choirs! My résumé spoke of my accomplishments: student recruitment (programs had tripled in enrollment), choirs recognized at the state and national levels, extensive background in musical theatre having performed over 30 leading roles. When the high school choral job opened up in a nearby city, I applied and took what would be my last position in teaching.

In my 46 years of research, I witnessed many changes. In my opinion, there is a direct correlation with these changes and the downward spiral of our educational system:

- Downgrading of dress codes for both students and teachers
- Teacher assessments
- Common Core
- Disruptive classroom behavior
- Technology driven teaching practices
- Shorter attention spans from students
- Parent roles running the gamut of helicoptering to complete absence

- Ill preparedness and immaturity of new teachers
- Administrators who could not or would not administrate
- Social media
- The increase of bullying, both in the perpetrator and the victimization of children
- Dismissing God and Christian principles
- School shootings
- Stem curriculum without the balance of the arts
- Higher student dropout

What are positive classroom norms? How do we manage today's children who feel entitled? Where do parents fit in strategizing? What is the role of the administrator? Do we mentor or do we change behavior by exhibiting a decidedly callous approach? By the conclusion of this book, I hope the reader can gain a better understanding of what it takes to become a successful student, parent, teacher and administrator. These four points of view (POV) will be addressed. My life journey encompassed all four. Where is your POV as you read on? I propose this challenge: through your own life experiences, are you willing to maintain an open mind and gain insight into points of view which differ from yours?

Student POV: This book speaks to you. Thus far the only role you play in this story is that of learner. You navigate between home life and school life. Some days you feel committed to learning. But let's face it. Many times, you barely get by because you are unclear about the purpose of attending school. Dedicated teachers serve you, but the opposite end of that spectrum exists as well. The great ones spend extra time in preparation. Their classroom management is fair and yet swift with consequences should poor behavior erupt. You glean knowledge from those educators because of a controlled environment. But the instructors who you have animosity towards also hold a place in the learning journey. They may be educators who appear tough and do not allow you wiggle room. Your half-hearted attempt to produce is unacceptable to these teachers. Those instructors are completely invested but do not personify "coolness." And then there are the teachers who are cool. They dress like you, use your language and pride themselves that you are their buddy. You know them as the teachers who give the easy "A". Their classroom decorum is nonexistent as well as their ability to disseminate knowledge. Are you really learning under the guise of a hip teacher? The ideal teacher embraces fairness, demonstrates infinite preparation, presents a demeanor of the consummate professional and grants grace when needed.

But for some of you, school, teachers, and friends never rise up to your expectations. You whine and complain, either by your own need to feel in control or by your parents, who model entitled behavior. If you cannot get your way or somehow you feel you haven't been treated fairly, you pout, try to get other students to support you, or run home to your parents to complain. Please read this book from a teacher's viewpoint. Walk in their shoes. No one said school should be fair, fun or easy. Not a teacher exists, including the ones you dismiss as inept, who rise out of bed in the morning and state to their mirror, "I am going to ruin my students' lives today, by grading them unfairly, so they want to quit." Stop treating those teachers whom you believe to be "unfair" with disrespect. The one who needs to change is you.

Parent POV: This book speaks to you. You have journeyed in two roles thus far: student and parent. Some of you may also be teachers. Being a teacher as well as a parent proves challenging at the very least. At school I tried to deal fairly, make calculated decisions, insure everyone's safety and multitask minute by minute. When I came home from teaching, the last thing I wanted to do was take time to be fair, make any decisions, insure the safety of my family, or function as a "supermom."

If you have always treated teachers with respect, then bravo! My mother was a teacher. When I came home with the injustices I perceived at school, she always asked first, "What did you do to get into this trouble?" My fourth grade teacher demonstrated daily her disdain for me. I would complain to my mother how I ended up the only one staying after school, when everyone in class misbehaved. My mother did nothing. When I told her my friends thought the teacher unfair to me, my mother just shrugged her shoulders. Did I want her to intervene with this teacher? You bet! Did I feel upset with my mother when she refused to defend me? Of course. But in those days, the teacher was always right so disgruntled parents proceeded slowly to complain. As a child, I resented my mother not fighting my battles. As a teacher, I wished parents would take a breath, step back and push pause on quibbling.

If you've ever hidden behind your computer and proceeded to write a three or four paragraph email to your child's teacher in a fit of rage, then promise you will never do this again! Your behavior is debilitating. Making assumptions about the transaction which took place between your child and his teacher, without fact finding or having a face to face meeting, provides no avenue to any solution. Today's seemingly precious children may not always interpret truthfully what happened in the classroom. If you do not possess the courage to speak to the teacher directly, then for the love of all that is human, stop writing it in an email!

A teacher in your child's life may truly need reprimanding. As you read further, a positive way to accomplish this will be discussed. Look at your position as a parent of one who mentors and not one who has the right to demand a teacher's dismissal.

Teacher POV: Where are you in your journey? If you are new to the profession, teaching children is just one segment of your daily routine and how you ultimately will be judged. Start now and muster your courage. There is life after every poor assessment, admonishment from an administrator and parent complaint. I will share events which could have discouraged me from continuing in this profession. Become your own hero in your story, and do not allow the naysayers to discourage you from doing what you love.

Do you consider yourself a seasoned teacher? If you are currently thriving in your assignment as well as in the past, count your blessings. Either a great administrator shielded you, or good karma escorted you! Be aware that the path to teacher retirement is strewn with loving and hateful children, caring and spiteful parents, mentoring and backstabbing colleagues, supporting and attack prone principals. If you have been defended by an administrator, do not take those actions for granted. It's likely you haven't seen that scenario many times, if ever, in your career!

Administrator POV: This book speaks to you. Do you conduct your school in a fair and just way? The law requires due process for your students. The law seems a little ambiguous on how your staff should be handled. Do you present as a Dr. Jekyll or Mr. Hyde? One day, swapping jokes with your staff and complimenting them. A few days later threatening that same staff with removal, shouting unfounded accusations, or speaking poorly of your staff in a department meeting?

You may have held three previous roles before your present position: student, parent and teacher. I would encourage you to draw from all three. Being tough on a child who consistently disrupts the classroom always nets a better result than saying to this same child, "I'm okay, you're okay." Reminisce your life as a student. The tough teachers and administrators who expected a better outcome became the ones who gained your respect.

From the teacher perspective, when you taught, how did you best respond to an administrator? Did you get better results with one who upheld consistent fairness, or the one who blindsided you, refused to fact find, and demonstrated his blatant distrust of you?

As you progress through this book, you will read anecdotes and actual quotes from my former administrators. What philosophy do you uphold? Do you mentor or manipulate teachers? Since you hired this candidate to teach on your staff, this teacher's success partially falls on your shoulders. As you point one finger toward the staff member in condemnation, remember three fingers always point back at you.

Enlighten and Enlist Others: A light gleams at the end of the tunnel, but is it an oncoming train? We need to initiate a national conversation regarding our educational system and even more importantly, the guaranteed fair treatment of those who serve our children. Otherwise our nation will continue to see teachers run over and run out of the field. One person can make a difference. If you see an injustice perpetrated on a teacher, be the voice of reason. Not just with words, but with actions. Such was the case of the following teacher.

A physical education teacher, removed from his position almost a month ago, fights for his life to return to the classroom. I have never seen such sheer determination, quality activism and dogged media attention. His students and parents demonstrated daily their determination to correct this injustice. They were victorious in their plan to win him back his job! Changing an educational system which reflects disparity in teacher pay, uninvested school boards, and unprofessionally run administrations will require constant activism by students, parents, teachers and administrators. Teachers are not an expendable commodity. Children's academic, social and emotional needs must take precedence over budgets and educational agendas, such as constant testing. I loved my life as a teacher. Over four decades of making joyful music gave my life definition and purpose. I regret nothing. So you want to rescue the teacher and save the child? Fasten your seatbelt and prepare yourself for tranquility, turmoil and thrill rides along the sometimes rocky road ahead.

CHAPTER 2: YOU CAN'T MAKE THIS UP!

Glass and Ceiling: The day dawned: a warm, basking in the sun of an open window sort of day. My teaching assignment covered seven elementary schools where I taught kindergarten through second grade general music. My other two colleagues and I posed as the musical answer to team teaching, since they taught music to grades three through six. That year we directed a multitude of holiday programs in those seven schools. The words "Merry Christmas" lost their luster by the fifth concert!

On this day, Maryann acted like every exuberant second grader. Her schedule dictated music class the last period of the day, so she grew excited to escape at 3:00 pm. Maryann seemed a little overenthusiastic as she physically plowed through her classmates to get to the door. Gently calling her name, I asked her to come back into the room and go out the door again in a more appropriate manner. Maryann decided she wanted nothing to do with that request. I used my bolder voice and commanded she come back and go through the door again. She turned belligerently toward me, stomped back into the classroom and proceeded to deliver an all-out temper tantrum. Flailing about on the floor, Maryann attempted to grab her face. At that moment, one of her classmates screamed, "Look out! Maryann's gonna throw her glass eye at you!" Yes, you read correctly. When I looked up, another child anxiously whispered "Maryann has a glass eye and she throws it when she gets mad." Her glass eye was news to me! In my divine classroom management style, I immobilized her arms with my hands so Maryann could not grab at the artificial eye. It was a   scene from a sitcom. Second grader wailing on the floor, teacher pinning her arms down with children getting ready to catch the glass eye should it become a projectile. All of a sudden, two large brown shoes appeared to my right. I slowly followed the pant legs up to a bespectacled man. The principal stood above me. He whispered, "Thank you Mrs. Baack. I will take if from here."

Teachable Moment: As an itinerant support staff, I was seldom notified about physical, mental or emotional conditions of my students. Always check with your counselors and special education staff to make sure you received all information available on any student, who may have issues in the classroom.

See Something, Say Something: I worked with a talented student teacher. Sitting in the back of the room, I recorded her responses as she instructed our first graders. The children sat on those sweet little chairs as Susan perched herself on the same small piece of furniture. Since she was trained as an opera singer, I thought the first graders would not accept or completely fail at matching the intensity of her voice. On the contrary, one child remarked she sang like a real lady! When Susan delivered the lesson, I noticed an odd quality to her speaking voice. It seemed as if she might gag. Did she possibly have a health issue? Susan looked determined to finish the lesson. She demonstrated a song and again, she uttered a sound similar to that of a 99 year old who might expire soon. As children departed, I inquired if she felt ill. Susan gave an embarrassed laugh and then explained. One of the children picked his nose. His finger made connection with a rather long string of mucus. The child's finger, with mucus attached, pulled the string of mucus about 10 inches from his nose. This young singer contemplated his next move for at least several seconds. With the child's back to me, I couldn't detect the problem but now I clearly felt the same gag reflex.

Teachable Moment: Always correct behavior which takes focus away from the teaching. Ignoring the bad and rewarding the good only experiences successful outcomes in an academic setting where students work independently. In a choral, general music setting, that philosophy failed. If you see poor behavior, say something immediately.

You're Fired! One semester the university contacted me about taking on a student teacher who faced issues dealing with her current cooperating teacher. I maintained the position of the positive Polly-Anna who believed I could help anyone. The first day Jenny reported to my school, she informed me she liked to play the game of "assassination." Everyone on her dorm floor put in a great deal of money. Each participant possessed a plastic paint gun with the sole purpose of eliminating the competition by "assassinating" them. The last one standing would win hundreds of dollars. Jenny worried someone would try to "take her out" while she taught at my school. I informed her it would be completely inappropriate for anyone to come on our campus and pretend to attack her with a gun. Jenny would prove to be a handful.

Within 15 days I typed four single spaced pages of documentation on her inability to act in a professional manner. At a competition, while seated in the audience, she stood up and directed our students on stage. Jenny could not will herself to stay on topic when presenting a lesson to the class. Her mannerisms seemed flighty, and her thought process scattered. Establishing eye contact proved a great challenge for her. My frustration rose as she could not take any constructive criticism. Then things moved from bad to worse.

Six young girls entered my office 15 minutes before school started. They asked to meet with me about a serious matter. It appeared our student teacher blurred the lines between herself and the students. Jenny captured the girls' attention upon gleefully encouraging them to watch a fellow classmate. Shawn appeared older than his years, good looking and well sculpted. Jenny emboldened the girls to checkout Shawn's unrestrained masculinity. I gasped. The fact these adolescent girls felt insulted by Jenny's behavior was admirable. When I looked into their faces, I could see they expected me to do the teacher thing and stop this behavior immediately.

When Jenny entered my office a few minutes later, I fired her. I told her to pack her food and family pictures into the large paper bag I provided for her. While the shock on her face promoted definite satisfaction, I could see she still didn't get it. When I shared with her the previous meeting with the girls, the look on her face did not fulfill my expectation. Instead she sneered, rolled her eyes and said, "Oh that." This led to my walking her out of my room. Every step of the way, I raised the intensity of my forced whisper. Never could she return! When she disappeared down the stairs, it occurred to me that my cooperating teacher job description probably did not contain the ability to fire student teachers.

I worked under a wonderful principal who preached we teachers needed to take responsibility and let him know immediately if questions arose from our actions. He did not like being blindsided. I found him in his office, explained about the firing situation, and then asked him what sort of chaos might ensue from my actions. With a kind smile, he quietly remarked this circumstance was indeed rare. He suggested I call the university immediately. The voice on the other end of that conversation seemed paralyzed with fear that I committed an unforgivable act of treason. Jenny's father, a well-known philanthropist, might decide to challenge my actions. This could cast an adverse light on the university. For several days, I waited for my phone to ring with accusations of unfairness. Nothing materialized from Jenny, her father, or the university. It all seemed to end there until the university newspaper heard of my actions and ran a story on it. In their research, they discovered Jenny's father used his influence to allow her to complete her student teaching in another city.

Teachable Moment: When the paper tried to contact me, my principal told me to make myself unavailable for comment. I obeyed. As long as my principal remained informed, I owed no one else an explanation. This experience taught me to keep documentation, communicate directly with my administrator, and take a moment to think before acting emotionally.

Brain Numbing Conversations: Teachers' conferences, at the secondary level were scheduled in the late afternoons and evenings. They were designed as a method to encourage face to face meetings with parents. Since all grades were posted online, why this necessity? For any questions, parents or students could email. Most who made the effort to attend conferences were parents whose children did well. Seldom did the parent of the failing child appear. And yes, a correlation prevails. Instead of using 21st century technology, my district insisted I sit in a large gym at a child's desk under yellow, glaring lights. In my early career, conferences operated on a schedule, which meant I knew what parent would come at what specific time. Since the 90's, parents, with no name tags, literally appeared out of nowhere expecting to hear an intellectual conversation about their child's progress. At the surface I appeared a willing participant in the conversation. But my overtaxed brain desperately strived to remember their child's name and achievement level. After teaching a full day and conferencing for an additional two hours, Jill Adams' mother approached my desk.

I conveyed her daughter needed to take an active part in class and try to sing out. Jill seemed shy and aloof. I wanted my students to experience music at its fullest. As I continued speaking how Jill seemed reticent, I could see no ownership to my portrayal of her daughter. When I took a breath, Mrs. Adams asked if I had the right child. Her highly verbal daughter talked too much in her other classes and loved to sing. I paused, looked at my roster and wondered how I possibly made such a drastic mistake. My 11 hour work day proved my only excuse. Then it dawned on me. There were two Jill Adams on my roster: one white, and the other African-American. In front of me was seated a Caucasian Mrs. Adams so I assumed her the parent of the white Jill Adams. As it turned out, her daughter was the African-American. Luckily her good sense of humor prevailed, and she found the moment amusing.

Other conference follies included a parent slamming her fist on my desk, raised voices, and even looks of consternation and righteous anger, displayed in this very public format by both teachers and parents. A rowdy five-year old child accompanied his parent and took at least 10 pictures of me with his mother's phone for five minutes while we attempted to talk about her older daughter's progress. Nothing like "click, click, click" to challenge my ability to speak in complete sentences.

Teachable Moment: The best way to facilitate communications with parents begins with conferences, said no teacher ever. I would suggest an email sent to those parents with whom you need to conference. Share with them your desire to expedite their conferencing experience. Try to schedule those conferences during an assigned time. Email the remainder of your parents stating if they did not receive a request to conference, their child was achieving at grade level or higher. Of course they could drop by during conferences, but they should understand you need time with those students/parents with real issues.

Clothes Do Not Make The Man: Thirty minutes into the rehearsal with my junior high school men's choir, I received a new student. His counselor dropped him off without much explanation. The defining culture of the 80's boasted extreme dress for many. But this young man exhibited a jaw dropping appearance. Steve wore heavy make-up, purple hair, and his leather jeans fit so tightly that he found climbing the stairs of my risers difficult. He sported a bold leopard vest which stretched around his ample stature. Every pocket contained a long chain connected to yet another pocket. Steve's appearance made it challenging for the class to mask their awe. As a teacher in the performing arts, I admired students who dressed outside the norm. Steve took his individual look to a new level of creativity. I quickly assigned Steve a seat and remarked how I admired his rocker look. The glare he shot in my direction disguised nothing. Steve displayed an attitude with a capital A.

Steve's membership to our choir would prove interesting, as we prepared for a patriotic music celebration. I proceeded with our class discussion about the National Anthem. Out of the corner of my eye, I could see Steve's hand shoot up. I immediately went into yoga breathing, which prepared me for any verbal onslaught. In with the good breath, out with the bad, I called on Steve. He spoke in a low, exasperated tone, "What if I don't like this country and I don't want to sing this song?" I told Steve I would like to visit with him in my office over the noon hour so he could share his thoughts. I assured the class Steve was NOT in trouble. I did so hoping this would stop any student-led hypothetical discussions on Steve's presence in our choir. The meeting was not about disciplining Steve for his outspoken manner. I genuinely wanted to hear his views on the subject.

He arrived at lunch looking disgruntled in that surly, roll of the eyes way which all teenagers mastered by age 12. He slumped down in the chair, looking at the floor. I told him I valued all students' opinions, especially those in opposition from my beliefs. I grew up as an outspoken teenager, and most of my teachers openly disliked me for it. As a teacher, I aspired to a different standard. My comment genuinely surprised him. In the next few minutes, Steve and I found common ground. When he shared some of the downfalls he witnessed with our country, I could not disagree. We came to the conclusion that when we sang the patriotic songs, he would be excused from singing. Men and women sacrificed their lives defending his right to make that decision. Steve transitioned well into our class and when the patriotic concert came, he performed every number. Did all my confrontations with students end so successfully? No, they did not. Acknowledging the fact young people nourish opinions different from adults allowed the sharing of those ideas, without prejudice, in a healthy environment. A sarcastic or demeaning retort from a teacher closes down any possibility of respectful discourse.

Teachable Moment: I honestly enjoyed visiting with students who held polar opposite beliefs from me. Modeling positive discourse became a great way to help the student feel heard and respected. Polarizing episodes began to dissipate, and in their place, an honest exchange of ideas. Today's society could learn from this one important aspect of human dynamics: agreeing to disagree is much healthier than hating and demeaning the other person for their point of view.

Bullying is Real: Leonard was a come to life Dickens' character. Like Steve, he joined our men's choir midterm, without much introduction from his counselor. Leonard stood at least six feet tall, with an extremely thin build, and shaggy facial hair. His dark skin seemed overshadowed with blotches of dirt. On his first day, he gallantly walked to the last row of risers, but his large feet betrayed him. They hooked onto vacant chairs, sending them crashing. A true testament to his arms and legs growing at twice the speed of his torso, common of most junior high students. He appeared as an orphaned child, dressed in shoddy clothing. I could sense our upper socioeconomic school would find it challenging to accept him. Unfortunately Leonard would face much worse than I imagined.

Leonard's attire reflected his demeanor and attitude. His face displayed a countenance of toughness, ready to fight anyone. Students sensed this immediately, and some decided to challenge his mere existence. One afternoon, I heard a loud commotion outside my third story classroom. About 50-60 students gathered below my window, shouting derogatory comments. I could not see the beneficiary of the shouting, but it concerned me that the crowd mentality moved towards violence. Leonard stepped out of the front door of the school to taunts, name calling and challenges to fight. I stood frozen, watching this unfold. Before I could even think of reacting, Leonard took off on a dead run with those 50+ students screaming behind him. It became a scene out of a horror movie. A desperate man child running down the middle of the street, with the lynching mob close at his heels. Before I could report what I witnessed, Leonard and the crowd disappeared from view.

The administration believed anything which happened off campus untouchable. I understood the legal ramifications, but this mindset would not help Leonard. Our administration's hands were tied and nothing could be done. Or at least that seemed the thought at the time.

The next day I canceled rehearsals, sat down with my choirs and held a discussion on how humans should conduct themselves. I expressed my sadness about Leonard's plight. One student shared the conclusion of Leonard's run for his life. The crowd chased him into the lobby of a retirement center, where he took refuge. Leonard hid there until the bullying group of students dispersed. My students decided to initiate a letter writing campaign to Leonard in hopes he could see this school as something other than the monster portrayed by the angry crowd. With high enthusiasm for affecting change, the students completed their letters by the next day. I read each one to insure appropriateness. In every teacher's life, clock stopping moments occur when he feels proud to be in education. This qualified as one of those junctures of character and unconditional love. The letters proved incredibly thoughtful and profoundly apologetic. Three days passed but still no sign of Leonard. I looked up Leonard's address and decided to deliver the letters personally. What I witnessed would become seared in my memory forever.

Most of our students came from middle to upper class neighborhoods. Yet one mile from school stood Leonard's house in disrepair, surrounded by a dirt yard. Crumbling front steps and a yard filled with clutter greeted me. A young, half-dressed child answered my knock. The garbage strewn floor did not captivate my first impression. No floor existed in the house! Five young children, standing on a dirt surface, dressed in filthy clothing, stared up at me. Then I saw Leonard, perched on a chair, looking incredibly sad. With no other chair in sight, I remained standing, confessing how sorry our choir kids felt about the disreputable behavior exhibited by the crowd. Leonard only nodded. I handed him the letters and told him he would find a safe place in my room should he return to school. He muttered something about not returning. I understood but I hoped he would give our school one more chance.

A few days later, Leonard appeared in the doorway of my classroom. From that moment on, my students insured Leonard found a way to finish his ninth grade year without further bullying. After he left our school, I lost track of him. Did all my lost souls end up with an amazing end story? Unfortunately they did not. A school counselor once warned me I could not save all the kids. Those proved prophetic words. I found it challenging not to reach out to every child in need. Even if I could not save every child, at least I learned to celebrate small victories along the way.

Teachable Moment: Advocate for the defenseless students! If warranted, choose drastic and unexpected solutions to further the cause. Your actions, more than clever posters or speech, will guarantee your room protected from harm. At noon, my classroom filled with students who needed to eat in a place of safety. Do not let fear stand in the way of demonstrating your fierce warrior inner self to your students. Your actions create an environment for children to learn, free of animosity.

Another Teachable Moment: Visit with the counselors at your school regarding the procedure of admitting a new student to your classroom. Never should a child be dropped off at a teacher's room with no introduction and no background shared. Ideally this should take place before class and not during class.

Painting the Target: Bullies are drawn to students who exhibit victim mentality. Whining, complaining children sometimes paint their own target on their back. Teasing, a natural banter between kids, begins innocently. When the teased child appears to wither and withdraw, the aggressor feels more empowered. I would encourage those "victimized" students (both in junior high and high school) to do the following: 1. When someone teases you, either laugh, agree or walk away. 2. If the teasing turns into constant harassment, then stand up to that person with a rehearsed verbal closure remark and walk away before a war of words ensues. Publicly crying or tattling to an adult only gives the bully more strength to offend. 3. If the bullying takes on a menacing nature, then time to get an adult involved.

We inadvertently created coddled youth with rubberized playgrounds, helicopter parents and a victim mentality. When a girl in sixth grade called me fat a number of times, making my life miserable, I gave her a swift shove to the ground. My actions startled not only her but myself as well. I told her no more teasing or I would beat her up if she continued. The next day she gave me a friendship ring and we remained friends throughout high school. Would I ever advise physical contact as a way to combat bullying? Of course not. Our son came home in tenth grade afraid to go into the locker room because older kids began shoving him up against the lockers. My husband and I encouraged him, if he felt physically threatened, he could defend himself. Fearful it could get him suspended from school since the rules did not allow for fighting back, he asked what we would do if he were suspended. We told him we would support the suspension and not give him any further consequences. Thankfully it never came to that. Perhaps the advice we shared gave our son the confidence to face his bullies. Kids with confidence (whether earned or fabricated) seldom, if ever, bear the brunt of verbal or physical abuse from their peers.

This Girl Is On Fire: One of the first things I learned as a teacher was never to leave my students unattended. On this day, adhering to this rule of maintaining constant vigilance paid off.

I rehearsed the altos while the sopranos, on the other side of the room, waited patiently. With my back to the sopranos, I continued to give the altos extra help. All of a sudden I heard "whooooshhhh." I turned toward the soprano section, only to see one of my singer's hair go up in flames. You cannot make this up. The flames grew to five or six inches in height. While I headed in her direction in what felt like a slow motion movie reel, she frantically pounded her hands on her head to put the fire out. Miraculously the fire subsided by the time I reached her. Now we contended with the debilitating odor of burned hair. As she pulled out tufts of hair and screamed, I gently helped her stand and sent her to the nurse, accompanied by another student. As she exited, the entire school heard her guttural scream echoing down two flights of stairs, "My hair is falling out!"

All teachers shared the same lunch time and were congregated in the staff lounge when I made my entrance. My principal looked at me, shook his head and said I needed to explain what happened earlier. I assured him I had not left the classroom and was fully in charge. Nothing came from his lips. The bizarre fire incident, which circulated throughout the building, clarified the snickering I heard from my colleagues as I tried to explain the sequence of events.

Why did the child light her hair on fire? She attempted to melt her eyeliner with her cigarette lighter. Encountering a low flame, she leaned over and pushed the flame to go higher. Her hairspray covered hair immediately caught the flame. Luckily, the damage to her hair was only esoteric since the hairspray burned instead. While she did lose some hair, by the next day I witnessed no physical damage.

It didn't end there. Her parent called the following day to chastise me for telling students her daughter's hair caught fire. No ownership came from the parent that her daughter started her own hair ablaze. The only anger expressed was against me for sharing with students. The audacity! I reminded the parent her daughter screamed all the way down two flights of stairs "My hair is falling out." It's always easier to blame the teacher.

Teachable Moment: The legal ramifications of leaving your classroom unattended could result in the loss of your job and/or a student experiencing serious injury. Find someone close to your room to cover your class in case of an emergency. Do understand you work with students who possess the capacity to act quite unpredictably.

The Piercing Problem: My junior high men's chorus appeared to be the class where so many interesting things transpired. The choir consisted of seventh through ninth graders. Some of the boys looked fragile and possessed angelic soprano voices. Others appeared as bearded men who turned every conversation into a sexual innuendo. In the 80's, men piercing their ears became in vogue. I preached that my young men should have the "all American" look which meant no weird hair, facial hair or pierced ears. It seems an archaic viewpoint in the 21st century, but those were different times.

I prepared those young men for the first concert of the year by going over the appropriate dress. When the conversation turned to the wearing of ear studs, an argument ensued. No compromise here as I played the "it's my concert and I am in charge" card.

That evening my men's chorus lined up and proceeded to the stage. I heard a tittering from the audience but didn't understand the implications. As those young men loaded the risers, I noticed all of them wore a pair of outrageous clip earrings: gaudy flowers, drop pearls and crystal earrings shown forth. Seeing those youthful male singers diligently seek out such creative jewelry presented me with great amusement. The all-knowing smiles on their faces made me appreciate their attempt at levity. My sense of humor remained intact, as well as my hearty horse laugh. After the moment passed, they took off their earrings and performed. I do not remember what or how they sang, but I do recall I felt accepted as a teacher. Music danced with exuberance inside my heart. My students trusted my reaction to their prank, and a mutual respect became established. I loved being a teacher.

Teachable Moment: Throughout my career, kids wanted to tease me in an acceptable way. Laughter earned the best response. I possessed a self-deprecating personality, which seemed affable in the face of teasing or good-natured pranking. Taking myself too seriously would not have generated a positive outcome.

That Baack Woman: In my highest auditioned high school choir, one of my young men carried the look of a 25 year old heart throb. Adam epitomized tall, dark and handsome. The girls giggled in unsuppressed admiration while the guys thought him coolness personified. Adam's personality demonstrated his incorrigible hatred for authority. Mr. Brown, Adam's father, believed Adam infallible. Thus Mr. Brown's reputation of threatening counselors and teachers was well known throughout the school. When I tried to discipline Adam for his surliness, it came as no surprise when Mr. Brown cornered me in my office, demanding I not attempt to speak with his son. With Mr. Brown invading my personal space, I smelled the strong aroma of alcohol on his breath. Rationalizing with this father would not prove successful.

Adam drew the final straw when he called the New York City sex line during a Christmas party at one of the student's home. The parents informed me about the incident, so I added this infraction to the mounting behavior documentation. I dismissed Adam from our choir at the end of first semester, believing his new schedule reflected he no longer sang in our choir. Unbeknownst to me, Adam pretended he still attended choir. When Mr. Brown spoke to me after several weeks, I informed him Adam no longer remained enrolled in my class after first semester. Mr. Brown's wrath would not be quenched.

Later that week Mr. Brown made an appointment to speak at the school board meeting. Our school counselor attended the meeting and shared the following: Mr. Brown entered the meeting intoxicated, with slurred speech and difficulty in standing. He proceeded on a rant about that awful choir teacher who dismissed his son from the choir. Mr. Brown constantly referred to me as "that Baack Woman." The counselor found it humorous. I did not. The board listened, then dismissed Mr. Brown and his complaint.

A few days later, in the middle of my last class, the door flew open as my principal whispered breathlessly that I needed to leave school immediately. Mr. Brown called the school just previous to this interruption, stating fervently he owned a gun and was coming to school to put an end to that Baack Woman. You cannot make this stuff up. My principal sent me home to an empty house, since my husband was out of town on business. That weekend, terrified, I hid in my home with our seven year old child. If teaching brought me this kind of threat, why should I continue? That occurred over 30 years ago. When those serious, potentially life altering things happened to me as a teacher, the good, positive actions of students, parents, colleagues and administrators far outweighed those challenging times. Having daily and sometimes hourly conversations with God to deliver me from harm became another way I dealt with the drama. I never heard again from Mr. Brown. The students fondly called me *Baack Woman* for the remainder of the year. I rolled with the punches and signed my communications as BW.

A humorous ending brought closure to this story. My students wanted to surprise me with a decorated cake at the end of the year. They copied one of my room posters for the baker: *Baack Woman: Think Positive.* They attempted creativity in their design with some letters written in yellow. Unfortunately, the baker did not perceive the yellow letters correctly and believed that the message was: *Baack Vermin: Thin Positive.* The students felt embarrassed about the resulting cake fail. Seeing no cause for awkwardness, I believed the cake brought a satisfying conclusion to a crazy time in my life as a teacher.

Teachable Moment: As I recount this story, I am now alarmed at how callously the administration chose to handle this potentially life-threatening episode. With the multitude of school shootings today, administrators should take every threat seriously. I must admit my guardian angels worked overtime throughout my career.

'Tis the Season: During the holiday season, most music educators experience fear of singing anything with the word "Christmas". The secular progressives argue no war on Christmas exists. They need to walk in the shoes of music educators. One of my colleagues added the piece "Let the River Run" to his repertoire. The song used the term "new Jerusalem". Jewish parents in his school took him to task. For three months he defended the music, behind closed doors, to attorneys, parents and administrators. In the end, the district supported him and all threats of filing lawsuits dropped. I asked him how his exoneration felt. Instead of enjoying the holidays with his family, he spent the time justifying his choice of literature. I could sense through the sadness in his voice, the ordeal overwhelmed him. I felt Music cringe inside me. My flame flickered and decreased in size that day. Singing Christmas literature could result in the same outcome. The line of parents, wishing to dismiss holiday music, lengthened to include non-Christian religious groups, agnostic, and atheist community members determined to prohibit Christmas music in the public schools.

No matter what kind of holiday program I designed, someone would object to the words Christmas, baby Jesus, the wise men or even the term "hallelujah". One year I decided to approach Christmas through gospel music, widely recognized as being a vital part of our culture. The concert contained a lovely first grade song called "Mary Had a Baby." My principal ran into my room (administrators seem to do this a lot when they do not want to deal with parents) and said one of our Muslim parents demanded to speak with me on the phone, now. The confrontational phone call reflected the 70's, before parents could attack a teacher and hit "send" in the 90's. Speaking calmly with the parent, I told her how frustrated I felt trying to find holiday songs which would not offend anyone. The previous year, the students performed no Christmas music. Instead they composed music to a popular book, which was a part of the curriculum at the time. This approach garnered fast disapproval from my Christian parents. In December, they expected a Christmas program. I suggested to the Muslim parent she head up a committee of Christian, Jews, Buddhists, Muslims and atheists, as a representation of our community. I encouraged her to have those parents design a December program so everyone could feel happy. To my amazement, she seemed pleased about the idea and assured me she would start gathering the committee that day. I never heard from her again. With no committee for guidance, I continued trying to make each year's program agreeable to all, while wondering who would complain next.

A few years later, while rehearsing my sixth graders for the holiday program, a professionally dressed woman entered my classroom. She nodded and smiled. Then she took a seat in the back of the room, with pencil and tablet ready. She proceeded to write down everything I said! This woman must represent the American Civil Liberties Union, thereby documenting me so I could be fired for teaching Christmas music. When I feel scrutinized, the tendency to preview everything before I speak consumes me. My speech became filled with "uh, well, maybe". The more I tried to articulate the lesson faster, the swifter the lady wrote. I should have stopped and asked who she was and what purpose she had in visiting my class. But I was in the middle of teaching a lesson to kids with a short span for listening. Stopping to ask the visitor to identify herself never entered my mind until afterwards.

I felt this itching sensation on my arms. I started to perspire. The itching persisted. I desperately tried to get relief but red welts, the size of silver dollars, appeared on both arms. Hives presented as a product of my discomposure. As soon as the class left, with courage, I asked my visitor who she was and her purpose in recording my lesson verbatim. The lovely lady introduced herself as the mother of one of my students. Hired as a new teacher for the next semester, and admiring my teaching skills, she came to observe the methods I used in classroom management. My arms became a testimony that the war on Christmas was real and every music educator lived a life in limbo from November through January.

Teachable Moment: Stop your task at hand and ask any person who comes into your classroom to identify themselves and state the reason for their visit. Make sure your school maintains a strict policy of whom may come into the building and what proper procedure dictates if this person wishes to speak with you. Even with a strong security presence, people (volunteer parents) may show up at any time and possibly generate a confrontation. Find out what recourse you have against these likely encounters. Put a plan in place should the situation arise, and then call security immediately.

REFLECTION QUESTIONS:

STUDENT

1. How do you deal with peers who look, think, act and speak differently than you?
2. How do you deal with bullying when you witness it?
3. How do you cope when bullied?
4. Have you allowed yourself to become victimized when teased?

PARENT

1. How do you deal with friends of your child who look, think, act and speak differently than your child?
2. How do you deal with bullying when you hear about it?
3. Has your child been bullied?
4. Have you given your child skills to use when confronted with teasing?

TEACHER

1. How do you deal with students who look, think, act and speak different from the norm?
2. How do you deal with bullying when you witness it?
3. Are you able to hand out consequences to bullies that have shown positive results? If yes, what are they?
4. Have you given your students skills to use when confronted with teasing?

ADMINISTRATOR

1. How do you deal with students who look, think, act and speak different from the norm?
2. How do you deal with bullying when you hear about it?
3. Are you able to hand out consequences to bullies that have shown positive results? If yes, what are they?
4. Have you given your students skills to use when confronted with teasing?

CHAPTER 3: A CHRISTIAN TEACHER IN TODAY'S SECULAR PROGRESSIVE WORLD

The Song That Started It All: The day I broke out in hives, believing the ACLU invaded my classroom preparing a brief to fire me, provided a comical outcome to my paranoia. However, I am more prone to believe John Lennon's definition: *Paranoia is just a heightened sense of awareness.* My decades of employment in the public school systems witnessed a questioning of my classroom practices and on some occasions, the choice of repertoire. I achieved a heightened sense of awareness under the scrutiny of the new secular progressive flames which caused my inner flame to radiate less. The attempt to remove Christmas music began innocently enough with one of the world's most favorite songs.

Imagine the final day of school, before a major winter break. The halls ring, filled with children singing holiday songs. An elementary music teacher leads the impromptu hallway concert. How could this innocent setting become the launch pad for removing Christmas songs from the public schools?

The final hours before any major break become dreaded ones. No child exhibits interest in learning a new concept. No teacher can muster interest in teaching one either. Our final holiday concert always made its appearance at the beginning of December, due to finals. That forced our choirs (and other non-academic classes) to fill two weeks with creative instruction before break. I tried showing holiday movies for a couple of years only to watch students sneak out of my class, bored with the day's plans. I would imagine our elementary music teacher looked at a holiday sing-around as an appropriate way to end the semester. Whether she chose the songs or allowed the students to choose did not matter. The students sang the song "Silent Night, Holy Night" and thus started the war on Christmas with a shot fired across the nation via an angry parent. I was warned about this case as a student teacher. Eventually the litigation made its way to the U.S. Supreme Court. The suit was filed by an atheist parent on behalf of his son. Take a moment and Google "Silent Night, Holy Night" and the U.S. Supreme Court. You will find six pages of different bans, lawsuits, court fights and arguments pro and con for the singing of this piece. Ironic this one piece could be so controversial. During a WWI Christmas truce between the British and the Germans, both sides agreed to put down their arms during the singing of "Silent Night, Holy Night." While this song brought about a truce in 1914, it started a war of words in the 1970's.

In the mid 1970's, the superintendent of my school district sent out a declaration: the words "Merry Christmas" were to be replaced with "Happy Holidays." It stemmed from a parent who ripped a silhouette of the three wise men off the main bulletin board at my school. How could one person's denial of Christmas determine this 180º change for the entire district? Why did one action result in the removal of all contexts of the Christmas cultural celebrations? The secular concept of public school Christmas celebrations had been in place for centuries. This yearly festival was the most celebrated event in the world! What harm or detriment to society did the word Christmas perpetrate?

My initial response was to visit with my pastor. With my strong sense of right and wrong, I believed he could intervene to stop this nonsense. He pointed out public school children, who wish to celebrate Christmas, could attend parochial schools instead. A disappointing response to parents who would not be able to afford parochial school education. I do not believe Christian parents understand the precarious environment enveloping their children in the public school system. In my opinion, no balance exists in representing Christian views verses the secular progressive agenda. A parent confided her son, enrolled in the high school World Religion class, became disillusioned with the class. Christian history only encompassed the evil intensions exploited in the blood and gore of the crusades. Students confided in me their concern about the fetus definition and representation in biology. The classic Big Bang Theory verses God's creation no longer merited discussion or even an argument. The general philosophical viewpoint, even expressed by some Christians, believed Christianity did not need, nor deserve fair representation in the public schools.

According to the National Association for Music Education: *the study and performance of religious music within an educational context is a vital and appropriate part of a comprehensive music education. The omission of sacred music from the school curriculum would result in an incomplete educational experience.* The association continues with their interpretation of the First Amendment: *The First Amendment does not forbid all mention of religion in the public schools; it prohibits the advancement or inhibition of religion by the state. A second clause in the First Amendment prohibits the infringement of religious beliefs. The public schools are not required to delete from the curriculum all materials that may offend any religious sensitivity. For instance, the study of art history would be incomplete without reference to the Sistine Chapel, and the study of architecture requires an examination of Renaissance cathedrals. Likewise, a comprehensive study of music includes an obligation to become familiar with choral music set to religious texts.*

The chorales of J. S. Bach, the "Hallelujah Chorus" from George Frideric Handel's Messiah, spirituals, and Ernest Bloch's Sacred Service all have an important place in the development of a student's musical understanding and knowledge.

Each time I approached any Christian oriented song in class, I always gave students the option not to perform it. I recall one or two times where that did happen. One student volunteered to turn the pages for our accompanist. Another student quietly walked off the stage during the performance of the song in question, then returned for the remainder of the concert. I celebrated the rights of those students not to perform. Occasionally parents encouraged me to insert different variations of "Silent Night, Holy Night" at the end of our December concerts. My earliest memories of singing as a child involved ending church services and concerts with this song. Directing it as an adult transported me back to those lovely evenings with friends and family. I wanted my students to have the same experience. It did not forward the precepts of Christianity, but instead musical memories were created.

Teachable Moment: Before introducing any religious song, I always asked my middle, high school and collegiate students their interpretation of the Supreme Court rulings on public school students singing Christian content songs. Many stated it was illegal, a message often promoted by teachers too afraid to allow those songs performed in public. I explained a religious song may be legally sung in the public school classroom, as long as no one felt coerced to rehearse or perform it. Service men and women fought for the student's right to withdraw from singing any questionable song. I wanted them to opt out immediately to avoid having an angry parent accosting me after the concert. Only one time in my career did a parent question my use of religious repertoire. I will address this under *Ratio is the Telling Factor*.

The Person I Am: My point of view plays an important role in the context of a Christian educator teaching in a secular progressive world. When I was a child, my parents brought me up attending church every week, taking part in the youth group and singing in the choir. I was baptized and confirmed but my mother didn't think I officially received the Holy Spirit. She scheduled a private immersion baptism at the local Baptist Church when I turned 14. I went through all of the protocol reluctantly, and my mother was correct. I knew how to pray and recite Bible verses. No knowledge yet existed in my mind how God, through the Holy Spirit, would manifest His presence in my life as a teacher.

At the age of 15, I attended a Billy Graham (1918-2018) rally held at a football stadium, with tens of thousands in attendance. Dr. Graham, one of the world's renowned evangelists, always attracted substantial crowds. At the end of the evening, I descended the stadium stairs, committed myself to Jesus Christ and started my new life as a Christian. Cynically, my mother doubted my sincerity, especially after two water methods and six weeks of dutiful confirmation. Christians believe the Holy Spirit whispers into the thoughts of man and opens his heart to a relationship with Jesus Christ. Until that evening with Dr. Graham, my receptors appeared closed to any spiritual conversation.

Living a rather sheltered life, it never occurred to me that other religions existed until my days in college. To my small-town shock, one of my college professors declared himself an avowed atheist. Ironically, he formerly served as a Presbyterian pastor. My foundation and beliefs felt challenged every class period, which made me both angry and curious. We held heated and heartfelt classroom arguments. Neither one of us altered our viewpoints. But the exchange of ideas, in an environment which encouraged opposing views, proved a positive one as I awakened to the world around me. Expressing my walk with Jesus Christ in a public school setting, however, felt uncomfortable. Evoking the names "God" and "Jesus" in repertoire produced a cringe factor with many of my students.

The Third Person: Early in my career, when Christian repertoire was introduced, I discussed the meaning of the lyrics in the third person. This approach avoided any kind of reference to my personal beliefs. One school district, which faced constant challenges with the use of Christian music, suggested only 25% of any concert program display religious content. They arrived at this formula through the support of both parents and teachers in the community. That seemed a reasonable equation. My concerts seldom included more than two or three songs which could be considered religious (see Choral Program Summary 2011-2014).

However, a particular verse from the Bible always resonated in the back of my mind. Matthew 10:33 (ESV) states, "Whoever denies me before men, I also will deny before my Father in heaven." In the 15th year of my career, I changed from third person to first person when presenting religious repertoire. When introducing any new religious piece, this was my statement: "I am a Christian. This is not a religion, but a relationship with Jesus Christ. If you do not feel comfortable about singing this music, please come and see me privately. This way we may find a mutually agreed upon compromise, of what you will do, while the rest of the class rehearses this song. I celebrate your right to opt out of the performance of this song. Please visit with me, as soon as possible, so your parents may attend the concert knowing this was addressed." I never faced a lawsuit, as in the case of the young music teacher, who led the singing of "Silent Night, Holy Night" before Christmas break.

Teachable Moment: Since the 70's I dreaded the holiday of Christmas in the public schools. When I took the high road and refused to admit the observance of this holiday encompassed a major part of my relationship with Jesus Christ, it never felt like an authentic response. Holding transparent conversations with my students developed a much better rapport, and Music danced. Happiness surged inside me. My teacher and personal life should not hold contradiction. Separating a teacher's belief system from the lesson plan will prove challenging, and in my humble opinion, inappropriate in today's call for honest disclosure and discourse.

Ratio is the Telling Factor: My one and only time of being challenged, regarding the use of Christian repertoire, happened when a disgruntled student took home a copy of a Handel piece. I placed the copies on a table, ready to be passed out at a future date. This singer took the music home and informed her mother she was forced to sing the song. Her mother never bothered to contact me or my administration. Instead the parent beat a direct path to the superintendent. When parents implemented that approach, there was only one intent: do the teacher harm. The superintendent requested my programs from the past five years. The district discerned my percentage of Christian/religious music to secular music through the following summary (along with hard copies of programs) which I submitted to the district:

Choral Program Summary 2011-2014

CONCERT DATE	Sacred Songs: Secular Songs Ratio
March 2011	0:18
May 2011	0:21
November 2011	1:19
February 2012	0:13
April 2012	1:18
October 2012	1:16
November 2012	3:19
March 2013* *spiritual, gospel, R & B concert	4:16
MAY 2013	0:19
DECEMBER 2013* *included a Chanukah song, Jewish song about the children who survived the Holocaust, a Jamaican Christmas song and a song in Latin	5:27
May 2014	0:22
Total:	15:208
Summary:	7% Sacred 93% Secular

The challenge, from the parent questioning my use of religious songs, confirmed I was not guilty of pushing a Christian agenda into the choice of repertoire. Over five years, only 7% of my music held religious content. This stayed far from the 25%, which at one time dictated the norm. The parent was told about the results and the case closed. Thankfully her daughter dropped my class. It demonstrated a wonderful example of a district fact finding and then supporting their staff.

A previous principal stated we teachers must possess awareness of the "captivated and captured" classroom. When I taught Christian repertoire, which could lead to some students feeling uncomfortable, those impressionable young people did not possess the wherewithal to refute my beliefs or leave the classroom. Teachers must achieve balance in their presentations and remain proactive in their classroom discussions. Secular progressive agenda teachers also must follow suit. In their presentations, does room exist for Christian students to add their commentary? Is Christian history or literature taught with an objective point of view? Are they taught at all?

Teachable Moment: KEEP EVERYTHING! This includes, but not limited to emails, templates, grades, tests, and documentation. When asked to produce five years of programs (20 in all), I was relieved all programs were safely filed away and were retrievable within minutes.

Religion vs. Relationship: A few years ago, a colleague came to me with a concern. A contentious conversation started in his class. It was "common knowledge" Mrs. Baack was a Christian and therefore would not put any gay kids in her choirs. The conversation commenced innocently between two students. The teacher interjected it was not an appropriate topic and tried to end it. The open debate ceased but not before it became established that Christian teachers, because of their faith, must hate gay students. The consensus? Mrs. Baack's religion prohibited her from accepting gay students into her choirs. When the staff member related all of this, I couldn't stop myself from laughing at this false precept. Over the years, many times my gay students came out to me first, when they began feeling comfortable in their sexuality. My students trusted me because I never took a stance in judging their decision. I loved my students, without prejudice.

I privately shared the view point of the two students with my openly gay students. They found it humorous as well. My choir personnel held open discussions when we traveled to insure our gay students roomed with those who felt comfortable with their lifestyle. I interceded on several occasions when I heard disgusting language used in reference to our gay choir kids. On one such occurrence, I instructed the battered student to come to me if he ever felt harassed again. I was not nor would I ever be that teacher who chose to ignore those malicious behaviors.

How did I rectify the false narrative about my faith and philosophy of selecting students for the choir program? I asked the teacher if I could use 10 minutes of his class time and address the issue. He granted my request and so began my explanation: I do not belong to a religion but instead I walk in a relationship with Jesus Christ. I shared Matthew 7:12: *Do unto others as you would have them do unto you.* I base my Christian faith on the concept of treating others like I wish to be treated, never judging others, lest I be judged. I do not possess the skills, wisdom, or discernment to repress anyone because our viewpoints differ. My charge is to love others unconditionally, which is a command found in every major religion.

Teachable Moment: This charge of loving your students unconditionally will prove the most difficult, as there will always be students who not only disagree with your style of teaching but openly treat you with hostility. When those students hurled unfounded accusations at me, treating them fairly and demonstrating no animosity took every ounce of unrestricted love. When I rose to the challenge of doing so, the emotional impact felt very empowering.

Know Your Audience! In theater, directors always preach to understand your audience. The same may be said about teaching. Where does your district stand with religious content in the curriculum? In a site-based school, will the administrators support religious content as you swim the abyss of what is appropriate repertoire or literature? Have you visited with a parent group to see what the community will support? Several years ago, I wanted my students to understand the Holocaust through Hebrew music. That study still remains one of my most incredible highlights as a teacher. Additional information regarding this event may be found in Chapter 12. When the community perceived my teaching was to encompass all cultures, they no longer questioned my choice of repertoire. Establishing trust with your students, colleagues, parents, administrators and the community will insure your success.

Teachable Moment: To assume public school administrators or the community don't have opinions about the delivery of religious content would be naive. Instead, be proactive and seek answers from them to insure you reflect their philosophies in your classroom.

Walk the Walk: Pam loved the Lord, or so she professed at the senior ceremony. The students loved Pam for her expertise as an instructor in French. Her ability to lead a public Christian life, in a school where student prayer groups disbanded and Christian history taught through the bloodied crusades, was exemplary. Her adoring students voted Pam as "Teacher of the Year". Her speech showed boldness in context, as she expressed her love for Jesus Christ and gave Him the glory for her achievements. Less than a year later, Pam would have an opportunity to not only talk the talk but walk the walk.

Pam sat on the principal's council, which made decisions weekly regarding how the school would move forward, which departments needed prodding and what teachers may need to leave. Pam initiated an off-the-cuff meeting with me and began with, "I hear you are retiring." Three colleagues, sitting in my office, assumed I would return the following fall. Holding this hypothetical conversation would not serve anyone well. Since my retiring was not the case, I suggested Pam and I discuss this privately. When we stepped into the hall, I assured Pam I had no immediate plans to retire. Pam asked if she could at least approach the colleague lying in wait to replace me, and let her know it could be a possibility. Because of Pam's Christian faith, I trusted she would walk in that path. I would retire someday in the near future, so I could not deny Pam having a hypothetical conversation with the eager colleague. Trust and hypothetical remaining the operative words.

Upon forced dismissal from this position, the casual meeting with Pam took on much more significance. If she kept my confidence, I might still teach at the school today. Pam eagerly wanted me departed so the hiring of this other colleague could be done expeditiously. It affected Pam's department, so she made the decision to move things forward, without my permission. Pam did not throw me under the bus. But she certainly slowed the bus down.

Actions do speak louder than words. To this day, I am puzzled how Pam justified her actions when she found out I was forced to leave the school. God does not grant me the right to judge her. Forgiving her became one of my greatest challenges. I expected better behavior from a Christian sister. Now comes my turn to walk the walk. I must find a way to grant her grace.

Today's secular progressive schools desperately need staff with a moral compass. If you walk in the Christian faith, do not feel discouraged by my issues. On the contrary, dedicate yourself to teaching with integrity and always keep the "walk the walk" principle as the guiding light. Never should a job, a colleague or a situation cause you to ignore your conscience in order to justify the means.

If you do not hold to the Christian beliefs, do not condemn those who do. Instead seek common ground and question if there is something you might learn from this colleague.

Teachable Moment: Keep your confidences and trust no one. School systems, mired in playing politics, need to rise above the gossip or "hypothetical conversations". Teacher should not feel compelled to pass along confidential conversations in order to survive the fray. Avoid the whispered discussions in a deserted hallway. Your adverse behavior not only affects your colleagues, but more importantly it is a detriment to the student community.

REFLECTION QUESTIONS:

STUDENT

1. Do you allow others to discuss their personal beliefs in the classroom?
2. If you profess Christianity, do you witness your faith being attacked publicly? If so, can you defend your point of view?
3. If you do not profess Christianity, how do you deal with Christian teachers and students?
4. Are you familiar enough with the constitution and Supreme Court rulings when it comes to public debate on Christian music and literature?

PARENT

1. Do you believe teachers and students possess the right to discuss their personal beliefs in the classroom?
2. If you profess Christianity, do you witness your faith being attacked publicly? If so, can you defend your point of view?
3. If you do not profess Christianity, how do you deal with Christian teachers and students?
4. Are you familiar enough with the constitution and Supreme Court rulings when it comes to public debate on Christian music and literature?

TEACHER

1. Do you believe students possess the right to discuss their personal beliefs in the classroom?
2. If you profess Christianity, have you witnessed your faith being attacked publicly? If so, are you able to defend your point of view?
3. If you do not profess Christianity, how do you deal with Christian staff and students?
4. Are you familiar enough with the constitution and Supreme Court rulings when it comes to public debate on Christian music and literature?

ADMINISTRATOR

1. Do you believe teachers and students possess the right to discuss their personal beliefs in the classroom?
2. If you profess Christianity, have you witnessed your faith being attacked publicly? If so, are you able to defend your point of view?
3. If you do not profess Christianity, how do you deal with Christian teachers and students?
4. Are you familiar enough with the constitution and Supreme Court rulings when it comes to public debate on Christian music and literature?

CHAPTER 4: CELEBRATING THE SPECIAL NEEDS CHILD

But Jesus called them to him, saying, "Let the children come to me, and do not hinder them, for to such belongs the kingdom of God." Luke 18:16 ESV

The Divine Miss Kay: The joy of working with Miss Kay will remain with me for a lifetime. Little did I realize this frail petite girl, wheeled into my classroom by her paraprofessional, possessed the ability to impact my life forever. I tried to communicate with her, but she would not raise her eyes in my direction. This precious child, scrunched down in her wheelchair, was buried in blankets. With only her sweet brown eyes giving a hint of a human being, she appeared swaddled in a cocoon of protection from the cold world.

In our first experiences together, Miss Kay never emitted a sound. In my shortsighted perception, she seemed a paralyzed, non-verbal child who entered into my class after it started and wheeled out before it ended. I greeted Miss Kay upon her late arrival, which elicited no response from her, not even a head nod. Her wheel chair could only fit in the back of my room. As I would make my way forward to continue, I could not have positioned myself physically farther from her. I would glance at a her occasionally, only to find her asleep.

Then the divine happened. One day, after Miss Kay's para wheeled her into the usual spot in the back of the room, I heard her utter a nondescript sound. She blinked, fully awake and looked around the room, as if seeing it for the first time. I stood in pure astonishment! When I greeted her and asked how she felt, she would not respond, but we did make eye contact for the first time. Several days later, to my amazement, Miss Kay let out the F bomb! Only then did I come to the realization Miss Kay could not only communicate, but she knew full well the impact of her words. I needed to visit with the special needs staff immediately.

Communication Is Everything: I would soon learn Miss Kay could control when and how she responded. Not unlike most teenagers her age! The special needs department began inviting me to meetings with Miss Kay's mother. Those meetings opened a new world for me. Why had no one taken the time to let me know how capably Miss Kay could function in the classroom? How could I have connected with this very special human being and not known she could communicate? At what point did I drop the ball?

Upon visiting with the special needs staff, we came to the conclusion better lines of communication needed to be established. I initiated a plan where the Special Education Department would communicate with me, face to face, about each special needs child in my classroom (anywhere between five to eight children). We also needed to help the choir program's general education population understand the capabilities and needs of those special children. Every semester, before the additions of the special needs kids to my classes, the staff would come for questions and an honest discussion with the singers assigned to the choirs. The students and I could ask what to expect from the special needs children, and in turn insight imparted on how we could best provide a safe, learning environment for them. The following points reflect the ever changing learning curve when working with special needs children:

- Some of the autistic kids proved themselves as highly functioning and could sing during rehearsals. A few of these children could also perform at the quarterly evening concerts. Many expressed qualities of beautiful voices while others sang loud and proud.

- A few autistic children (severe cases) needed more attention where a carefully thought out approach yielded best results. Specifically our general education students were encouraged not to laugh at the special needs kids' antics or comical outbursts. Two additional directions were no physical contact with the special education students (for those prone to punch) and no unwarranted attention when our special children lacked focus.

- One of the greatest benefits of teaching special needs children was the general ed population understood they could not exhibit unfocused behaviors. Any negative conduct geared toward the rehearsal at hand proved a deterrent to the learning environment for both the special needs and general education population.

- The special needs children, due to pre-class personal hygiene care, generally could not make it to class upon starting time so when they did arrive, we would stop everything and greet each child by name. With the verbal kids, the singers in the class would ask them how they were doing. If they did not reply, I would get closer to them, establish eye contact and encourage their response. Thumbs up became our agreed classroom sign of approval to reinforce the efforts of our special children.

The rest of the story with Miss Kay? She learned my name and with a deep, out of character voice, she would shout at me BAAAACCCKKKK, one of the sweetest sounds to hear! Miss Kay began to appear in my classroom without the multitude of blankets, hat or gloves. She seemed a butterfly, morphing out of her cocoon.

I shall never forget when Miss Kay sang the *National Anthem* in class by herself. As she hesitated a few times, I helped her fill in the blanks. Hearing her sing filled my heart with joy. At her next IEP (Individualized Education Program) meeting, I asked her to sing if for everyone in the room. By the end of the song, not only was I choked up but so were the people who were assigned to her team. Teaching is a calling and I am blessed my life crossed the paths of these exceptional children.

Teachable Moment: I made a big mistake in not initiating conversations with those staff members who possessed the most knowledge about the abilities of their students. I wanted our choirs to be more than a "drop off" class for those children who could not achieve success in an academic environment. Never teach a day without knowing the capabilities of your special needs students. Do not accept the written explanations without getting to know the child first. Make it your goal to provide an active participation classroom instead of one for only observation purposes.

This Is Not Carnegie Hall: My elementary students eagerly prepared for their first concert. As performance time approached, I frantically looked for my music and a music stand. One of my perceptual sixth graders looked up at me and said, "Mrs. Baack! This is not Carnegie Hall!" I often thought about cross stitching that worthy advice and hanging it over my piano.

I often would refer to the sage Carnegie Hall reference when including special needs children into the choral experience. Edward proved no exception. Autistic, with skills to communicate, he demonstrated a profound love of music with a larger than life baritone voice. Orphaned as a baby, Edward's journey presented lots of difficulty. His adoptive parents knew full well their lives would contain incredible challenge and unconstrained love at the same time.

As with many special needs children, medications could make their lives easy or very difficult. Edward rode a roller coaster of emotions, due to his meds. He could punch a staff member and then within minutes of the aggression, sing angelically with his resounding low-pitched voice. We designed a united plan to give him a positive experience in choir. Helping him control his flailing arms and constantly moving legs became an integral part of that instruction. Relished moments of success needed celebrating, but afterward Edward would squeal with delight, flap his arms uncontrollably, dance around the room and appear unable to regain his composure. The morning rehearsal of the evening concert, Edward tried diligently to stand still and sing. His peer helpers loved assisting Edward and they gladly guided him through the process of standing still. One helper would gently take Edward's arms, when they took flight and tenderly pull them back to his side. Edward loved this helper so he willingly allowed him to bring his arms back down to an acceptable position.

The evening concert lifted off like a helium balloon, each choir's performance soaring higher and higher. Edward's class lined up on stage, and he appeared calm and relaxed. During the first song, Edward fought his body's excessive energy with all his might. Every ounce of strength Edward possessed charged on all pistons as he tried desperately to stand still. The second, more upbeat song began and Edward's body took off. His helper tried, with no success, to calm him. The students on stage continued singing but looked paralyzed with fear and embarrassment. Everything we encouraged Edward to do, he lost in this moment of jumping and flinging his arms to the music. Then came that God whisper. I motioned to one of my helpers to continue conducting the song while I walked up to the third riser and joined Edward.

He and I must have looked like quite a pair. We sang and bounced, moving our arms in synchronization and kicking out our legs. My students looked horrified. I encouraged them to collaborate with Edward and me. By the end of the song, most of the students joined in the "Edward Jig." The ensuing applause deafened as the audience showed their appreciation. God helped me decide, in a heartbeat, we could learn something about the true joy of singing if we became more like Edward. Years after, parents would remind me of Edward's "performance" and how it proved the highlight of their child's choral experience. When they shared how the experience affected them, some even choked up in describing the emotional moment of the presentation. Edward taught us the uninhibited jubilation of singing held far more importance than concert decorum.

That same year I asked this non-auditioned choir, without Edward present, if they wished to participate in the state choir competition. I pointed out we could go without Edward and that would be fine. I wanted my choir to compete and have a good chance for a high score. My students admonished me for even thinking about not taking Edward. They unknowingly hurt my feelings by accusations of prejudice but inwardly, I felt very proud of their response. Edward accompanied us to the state competition. He moved around during the serious music, flailed his arms during the upbeat portion and sang off key. I could see that it did not bother the choir so I decided it should not bother me. We ended up with an *Excellent* rather than a *Superior* rating. One of the judges took me aside and complimented me for bringing a student who appeared challenged. I felt embarrassed by the compliment for if it had been up to me, Edward would have stayed home. It is important to celebrate those times when teachers must learn important lessons from their students.

Later in my career, I was awarded a plaque and a generous stipend for my work with Down Syndrome children. When the parents of Julie stopped my concert to give me the award, I felt uncomfortable with the recognition. Julie did so much more for me than I ever did for her. She taught me how to demonstrate love unmitigated, remove the learning ceiling, and always allow for creativity when working with special needs children. Julie's senior project reflected a semester long compilation of arranging music and singing. I helped record a CD for her and it sits on my shelf as a constant reminder to never limit my expectations when it comes to learning.

Alex, Cindy and Ben taught me outcome-based assessments did not hold as much importance as making students feel welcomed in my classroom. When I addressed them by name, asked about their day and spoke of their remarkable qualities, the classroom transformed into one full of productivity and authentic love for one another. Cindy became my student assistant during her senior year. I wished all my student assistants followed directions and tried as diligently as she.

Teachable Moment: Avoid rigidity in your instruction and always have a plan B, C or Z ready when working with special education children. Do not allow these children to sit on the sidelines and merely observe your class for social purposes. Even the profoundly challenged children appreciate your hand on their hand, your verbal greeting and taking time to create an atmosphere of unlimited patience and love. Our special kids not only felt accepted, they thrived.

Plan "D" Works! Do not give up on your first few attempts of reaching out to challenged children. Kelly, an autistic child, loved to sing but her social skills proved arduous. She came dressed in an oversized coat, with a large hood covering her head, as if to hide from the scary world outside. She possessed a beautiful voice, not just sound in pitch, but truly the voice of a divine being. I wanted desperately for her to achieve success in singing. Our advanced classical choir remained the only class her schedule would support. We implemented the usual format of making sure those students understood Kelly's abilities and needs. The choir seemed prepared to take on the role of mentor.

Unfortunately Kelly's perception of pitch wavered according to her emotional state. For three weeks, this award winning, a cappella choir tried diligently to maintain patience while Kelly sang with them. Adding a wavering pitched voice to an a cappella setting never allowed Kelly to feel successful, as she could sense the other singers' frustrations. One of my leadership students came to me privately, apologized for speaking out, and begged me to release Kelly from their choir. I appreciated students who would come directly to me with a concern, so I wanted to honor her request. I proposed a compromise where Kelly would listen to the choir perform and then give them ideas for singing better. Kelly saw through my charade. She became highly agitated, left the room with her para and never returned. We tried getting her to sing with our non-auditioned choir, but she never appeared happy in that environment. An episode in another classroom setting seemed to trip her anxiety into an even higher state of flight. Kelly would not return to school for months.

A happy ending did come to pass. When Kelly eventually returned to school, I set up a plan through the advocacy of Kelly's para. Kelly held her own private karaoke days during my plan period. My student assistant would set up the projector with the words on our large screen and I would pull up YouTube karaoke tracks. Kelly sang confidently into the microphone. Her voice resounded throughout the empty rehearsal hall. Kelly found her voice. Not just the voice which loved to perform, but the voice which emboldened her to rejoin the frightening world she hid from all those years. It was thrilling to see Plan D implemented with a favorable outcome.

Make That Meeting: If you have a family member or know a friend in the teaching profession, you probably heard the complaints about too many meetings. Teachers feel overwhelmed with required meetings throughout the week and sometimes daily. However, effecting a concerted effort to attend meetings, where a child's educational experience is evaluated, should always hold the utmost importance. Those teachers, deciding not to attend, missed the opportunity to speak with parents, which altered the successful outcome of the meeting.

Face to face meetings became the expected format for IEP and 504 meetings (Individualized Education Program and an anti-discrimination, civil rights statute which requires the needs of students with disabilities to be met as adequately as the needs of the non-disabled). Designed for the child, their parent and teachers, the discussions presented large quantities of information, revolving around how to better facilitate the learning experience. Social workers, district health personnel and other professionals attended, as they would continue to work with the child post high school. In music, a path always presents itself for every child to find passion, love and most importantly success. To see a parent's face light up with pride when their child experienced success in school always felt like a treasured moment. I received affirmation from the Special Education Department, the parents and support staff, while my own department seemed on the ready to have me exit. Working with the special education staff became the one and sometimes the only place I felt validated as a teacher.

Teachable Moment: Whereas most of the other meetings I needed to attend could have been accomplished in an email, I looked forward to the IEP and 504 meetings. I felt honored to be asked to come and share. On those days when I received a request to miss part of my class to attend a meeting of this nature, at first thought, I would begrudge the time missed from my classroom. By the first couple of minutes of the meeting, however, I knew my presence balanced the challenges of teaching a special needs child with the good news this child felt successful through a positive experience in choir.

Who Really Benefits? Throughout my many years of teaching, a sustained debate persisted (and still persists) about how and why special needs children should integrate as much as possible with the general education population. When I began teaching over forty years ago, children who were in special education were never a part of the classroom. Their educational space consisted of a room or two down an unpopulated hallway. You would see those children occasionally, but no real interaction took place.

Fast forward a few years, Special Education Departments began utilizing peer helpers. A few selected general ed children would be chosen to help assist the special needs child. The special education room still remained distant from the other classrooms, but at least an outreach became available to those students who possessed a heart for working with remarkable kids.

My early 70's student teaching never addressed any pedagogy regarding how to instruct children who could not function in a usual classroom. I spent my first decade of teaching without experiencing special children in my classrooms. In the 80's, only highly functioning special needs children were allowed into the classroom. If I thought that prepared me to work with special education, I was certainly misguided in my assumption. Highly functioning special needs children possessed social skills and ability to grasp some concepts within the same spectrum as the general ed population. While the hearing and sight impaired child presented a different challenge, for the most part I did not change much of my teaching to facilitate special needs children in my room.

In perfect honesty, I sometimes resented those problematic children's very presence in my classroom. I felt challenged on how to develop activities for those kids. Was the Special Education Department using the choir program as an easy way to fulfill the state's requirement for classroom enrollment? I felt inundated with children who prohibited the forward progress of my gifted students. It all came to a climax one semester when eight special needs children, eight peer helpers and four paraprofessionals joined a choir of 20 general education students. Our room became so crowded with kids, wheelchairs and backpacks, the fire code for occupancy stood in question. I wanted to be the teacher who could do it all, but this situation became draining. Then God allowed me to see the bigger picture.

To my amazement, the growth of the special needs children did not even compare to the profound maturation of my general education kids. I felt assured those talented singers would be put off by having children in their choirs who could not participate at their level. I could not have been more wrong. My talented singers became the leaders who would take time to do a side hug with a child who could barely respond. Special needs kids' presence in the classroom did not impact how quickly we learned music. I believed all of us felt a secret pat on the back when we could achieve a great rehearsal even though Billy or Susie experienced a sudden outburst or insisted on walking around the room. The Special Education Department and I did strike a compromise about our highest competing choirs. We agreed those choirs would not prove appropriate for a special needs child. Even that compromise, modified on occasion, presented great success strategies. Jimmy was assigned to our award-winning Jazz Choir, where no place existed for him to sing due to the complexity of the music. He would rock back and forth to the beat of the drums as the students rehearsed. One day, he walked over to the drummer as class drew to a close. The same idea popped into the minds of the para educators, the drummer and me. We handed Jimmy the drum sticks, and our student drummer guided him on how to keep a simple beat. One of the para's videotaped the stirring moment for Jimmy's parents. And God and Music within me smiled. I felt my fire burn bright that day.

Teachable Moment: Embrace any opportunity to work with special needs children. When I experienced those moments of feeling overworked and underpaid, I would look at my special kids and realize how truly blessed I was wearing the title of teacher. Then an epiphany came to me. What would heaven be like when my special needs children and I reunited? We would see each other for the first time with unbridled euphoria! Every child, who went through endless struggle in his earthly body and mind, would display a completely healed heavenly body and mind. There would be no need for wheelchairs, walkers, or special accommodations. My special kids would smile, speak articulately and embrace one another. They would chatter of their gratitude for the opportunity to make music in a classroom void of prejudice. What a wonderful reunion!

REFLECTION QUESTIONS:

STUDENT

1. Have you taken classes with special needs students? If yes, how do you rate the experience?
2. Is there a peer helper position for special needs students at your school? If yes, would you consider volunteering?
3. Would you contemplate a career in special education?

PARENT

1. Have your children attended classes with special needs students? If yes, how do you rate their experience?
2. Is there a peer helper position for special needs students at your school? If yes, would you allow your child to volunteer?
3. Would you encourage your child to consider a career in special education?

TEACHER

1. How would you assess the special education program at your school?
2. Do you allow special needs children in your classroom, even if it is only for social reasons? If not, why not?
3. If a special needs child can function at some level, how do you bend your curriculum in order for that child to feel successful?

ADMINISTRATOR

1. How would you assess the special education program at your school?
2. Do you allow the general education population to act as peer helpers with special needs kids? If yes, how would you rate their experience?

3. Does your Special Education Department need anything specifically from you? If so, what could you do to insure this department's success?

CHAPTER 5: PARENTING 1.1

Hear, my son, your father's instruction, and forsake not your mother's teaching, for they are a graceful garland for your head and pendants for your neck. Proverbs 1:8-9 ESV

Parental Assault: The parents of special needs children, in general, championed their children's teachers. When parents of my general education children acted out adversely, I wished they could emulate their parental counterparts of special needs children. The role of encouragement plays significantly in not only children but also their teachers.

Picture a lovely afternoon with an entire choir program (140+ students) gathered at the local restaurant to display their talents. An opportunity to perform at this local establishment (with 40% of the dinner earnings going directly to our program) appeared to possess all the excitement of a live performance. The order of soloists, small groups and choirs painstakingly planned by the student leadership. Amazingly the restaurant filled to capacity with parents and friends of my students. The operative word "capacity" would ultimately determine the evening's destiny.

Unfortunately, this eatery failed to plan on the size of the event, as evidenced by the fact the wait staff became overwhelmed within the first 30 minutes. As our talented singers performed in front of the 150+ diners, parent complaints wafted through the evening's air. It became obvious timely submission of drink and dinner orders failed for many. The gentle rumblings turned into loud conversations between disgruntled parents and the waiters. I apologized to the parents whenever time would allow me away from the program. Most smiled, stated they were fine and would deal with the situation. I started to relax and enjoy the multitude of presentations when all hell broke out.

With an agonizing look, Rita, one of the mothers, waved me to come over. She stood nervously off to the side of the stage. Confusion swept over me as she hoarsely whispered the owner of the restaurant demanded her to leave immediately. Two questions engulfed me: how do I stop this situation from disrupting our performing students, and what nonsense did this parent engage in to have herself extracted from the restaurant? I approached the manager, with Rita in tow, to make the inquiry. The owner hissed the accusation that Rita told his wife, the co-owner of the restaurant, to "F" off and Rita must leave the restaurant immediately. She amplified her assertion about the lack of service. With patience demolished, he walked away shouting at her to leave now. The drama rose to a new height as he threatened to call the police. I gently took Rita by the arm, whispered in her ear she should leave as this scene exposed her daughter to much embarrassment. Rita pulled against my restraint and attempted one more round with the manager. I finally talked her into exiting the front door. After Rita made her egress, I sought the owner's wife and expressed regret for this parent's abusive behavior. Two other parents approached me, unsolicited, only to report Rita behaved badly the entire time. Meanwhile, my singers continued performing without me!

The three hour event concluded without further disruptions. Wait staff began the clean up process. I approached every waiter and apologized if they experienced the brunt of any parent anger. They all reacted graciously and said everything was fine. I located the manager and again apologized for Rita's behavior. According to the manager, her wrath made an unfortunate encore appearance.

Rita reentered the restaurant within minutes of my escorting her out, picked up a square alert pager and hurled it at the assistant manager, dashing him in the head. The manager retorted he would summon the police, and file assault charges against Rita. Disheartened and incredibly embarrassed by the entire situation, I remained speechless. Planned as a lovely evening for my students, the event turned out to be a dismal failure. I do not remember how much money we raised. The evening's chaos created by the actions of one parent left me in a state of hopelessness.

Later that evening, instead of coming home and gaining some much needed decompression time, I documented the entire episode and emailed it to my principal. Ironically, no charges were leveled at the parent by the police and the incident never reported to the administration by the restaurant owner.

Teachable Moment: I never regretted trying new approaches to fundraising, even those which failed. Foreseeing the issues of our restaurant concert couldn't even make my "Queen of the Worst Case Scenarios" hypotheses. One of my favorite sayings is: you get to choose those experiences you wish to repeat. I chose never to fundraise again by performing in a restaurant.

The Entitlement Factor: Many more anecdotes exist regarding incredible misbehavior of parents. Teaching, if only dealing with the child component, would be a much more enjoyable vocation if the adults didn't feel compelled to manipulate the scenario. The parental expectations of entitlement, which stymies the emotional, social and educational growth of children, could be one of the main reasons for the fragmentation of school systems. If administrators remain afraid to give voice to the word "no" to an entitled parent, which many times was my experience, how can teachers function in these no-win circumstances? The entitled children do not learn this behavior in a void. Their parents model this victim mentality as well as the inability to follow any prescribed rules. The entitled believe they deserve things, either due to their socioeconomic status or the boulder on their shoulder. "Deserve" remains the key word:

- My child deserves to sing the solo.
- My child deserves more playing time on the field or on the court.
- My child deserves to receive the highest grades.
- My child deserves to be treated with high regard, in spite of his negative actions.
- My child, because of social status or learning ability, deserves to disregard rules which other children must follow.
- My child deserves the best from life, as failing is unacceptable.

Did those attitudes originate from high school parents? No. Those ideas manifested themselves when children began in elementary schools:

- When I taught sixth grade music, a parent complained to the principal her child should get the solo.
- With today's club sports, young boys and girls begin playing competitive sports starting at the age of four. Games become vitriol with parents shouting at officials and coaches. Unfortunately, that mindset crept into the schools. Parents now feel emboldened to demand special treatment in performing arts, sports and academics.
- Parents, discovering their elementary child grouped in a lower ability status curriculum, place pressure on the

teacher and administration to change the assignment. It should come as no surprise some parents do not necessarily hold real interest about the progress of the child's education. Simply put: they need their child placed in the highest group, even as early as first grade.

Cocooning children at an early age creates negative learning environments through high school and college. At the graduation ceremony, the principal remarked a large percentage of the graduating high school seniors enjoyed a 4.0+. When I asked another faculty member how this could be the case, she asserted teachers in the feeder middle schools, forced by parents and administrators to give higher grades, made peace with that decision in order to keep parents happy. The same philosophy of distributing unearned grades continued at the high school. College campuses added "cry rooms," perhaps to mollify the young adult, who for the first time, may not have received what they thought due to them.

Teachable Moment: Not only should you allow your child to fail, you should celebrate it! Even if the perceived failure resulted from unfair selection or grading, supporting children in the how to's of overcoming disappointment is paramount to their development. Biographies are filled with scores of professional athletes, actors and musicians who failed in the early part of their careers. Most succeeded with hard work and perseverance. Thankfully no parent, teacher, administrator or coach felt pressured to change the sequence of the events directing their young lives. Colin Powell said it best: *There are no secrets to success. It is the result of preparation, hard work and learning from failure.*

Strike One: A student initiated a petition seeking to change how I selected soloists. He impertinently passed the document around during a presentation by a guest speaker. When I discerned his covert actions, admonished him and took away the document, my administrator would not support my actions. The boy's mother scolded me in several spiteful paragraphs, sent of course, in an email. At the EOY, the admin team waved this in my face as another example of my ineptitude.

Teachable Moment: Entitled parents must be stripped of the power to dictate classroom decorum or discipline. They are encouraged by administrators who feel fearful of telling them their children are in the wrong. Until administrators once again discover their backbone, this systemic problem will continue to discourage anyone from remaining in the teaching field.

Strike Two: When a student didn't make the talent show, I counseled the inquiring parent this situation could illuminate positive strategies of accepting disappointment. Patient phone and email responses appeared to make these parents even more hostile. Both parents dispatched three disparaging emails with the intent to wound me. Accusations of incompetency railed against me, as their son <u>deserved</u> to sing in that show. They arranged two meetings with the administration in order to circumvent me and have their son placed into the program. Whereas this did not end up happening, never once did the administration make any attempt to defend me. Instead, they cross-examined my audition rubrics and philosophy. My rubrics and publicized audition policies produced no affirmation by the administration. At my EOY, this supposed indiscretion on my part confirmed I possessed a serious problem of playing favorites.

Teachable Moment: At the beginning of every term, a performing arts teacher and coach should conference with the administrator to insure there will be support available when making decisions in auditions or sports tryouts. Perhaps a signed document, agreed upon by both parties, can serve as the best insurance against an ineffectual administrator who could possibly turn any parent complaint into questioning the integrity of the teacher or coach and using it in a final evaluation.

Strike Three: For the past two years, I accompanied my choir students to New York City to tour the city, attend Broadway shows and have workshops with Broadway actors. This excursion, open to all students, not just upperclassmen or advanced choirs, provided a once in a lifetime experience. One parent emailed me with a concern. Discussing the NYC trip in class came across as unjust, since her daughter could not attend. She suggested I spend time after school and not use class time to disseminate information regarding the trip. This proved impossible, since most of our students bussed to campus and could not stay after school. The mother also added she wanted nothing to do with fundraising. I asked the parent for a sit-down meeting. She never responded.

Much of our fundraising helped purchase performing attire for our students in need. While this parent would not support fundraising, it did not prevent her from requesting and expecting the choir department to outfit her daughter for free, since the family experienced challenging times. Of course at my EOY, this too raised concerns. Asking for money (fundraising) deemed an inappropriate use of class time.

Teachable Moment: When visiting with an administrator, all conversations pertaining to your actions should be transmitted by email. Documentation validity, while a needed component, requires email conversations supporting the discussions. Communicate through email an understanding of the actions and seek the administrator's reply verifying the outcome. Months after any discourse, no one recalls the exchange of comments unless documented. With the ever present dysfunctional administrator and entitled parent, keeping tabs on conversations helped to define what actually transpired.

Strike Four: A parent wanted her son to study for the SAT test and not attend the required Friday concert in October. The concert dates and attendance requirements, published in August, explicitly defined how concerts would be graded. Illness or family emergency always remained excused. Since wishing to study on a Friday evening could not possibly be accepted as an illness or family emergency, I would not excuse the absence. The parent complained to the administration about my unfairness. Dave, my administrator, would not support my grading (even though published on the website) so I allowed the student to perform for only his portion of the concert. The student received points for 30 minutes out of 90 minutes which gave him a "B" for the concert. His overall choir grade still remained as an "A" but the mother remained dissatisfied. She showed up in my room unannounced, sat in the back while I taught, and then after the class exited confronted me in tears. In the accusing conversation, the mother remarked if I truly believed in Christ, I would certainly hold a better understanding of why she needed her son excused from the concert. My Christian beliefs scrutinized over grading procedures? I stood my ground and would not change my grading procedure, but I verbalized my sympathy for her frustration. Her next approach to pressure the grade change came in the form of "no one would be the wiser." I explained that would not be fair to the other 150 students, who set aside the evening to perform on the concert. We agreed to disagree and she left. And yes, that episode appeared in my EOY as well.

Teachable Moment: Never, ever grant permission to a parent for a one on one conversation in your classroom if there appears to be a veiled agenda! Should any conversation turn negative, stop it immediately and refer the parent to the administration.

Five and You're Out! Four parental accusations out of 150+ parents might be construed as a triumphant year. The fifth parent, Mr. Jones, presented the final straw. But first, meet a young man, who to this day, does not realize the full role he played in ending my career.

Lon, a talented and passionate Korean-American student, with a personality which entered the room before he did, began his journey with me three years before mine ended. His handshake and direct eye contact demonstrated a natural leader. When Lon auditioned for choir, he impressed me by his ability to sing and read music. An early music education escaped Lon as most of his knowledge came out of self teaching.

The first concert of the year held high anticipation so excitement pervaded the halls. My student leaders gathered in my office an hour and half before call time to insure all preparations completed for our debut concert. My office phone rang with Lon on the other end stating he did not have transportation to the concert. In my teacher voice, I declared my displeasure. Why the lack of communication before that point in time? As I heard him utter the words of "living in a homeless shelter downtown and the family's only car broke down," my harshness convicted me. In a voice softened by the nature of Lon's predicament, I turned to my student leadership and described the situation. Before I could problem solve, two students ran out of my office shouting they needed Lon's address texted to them so they could pick him up. Lon made it to the concert in plenty of time due to the actions of those students.

From that time forth, my kids and I undertook the task of picking up Lon from the shelter. Shortly after Thanksgiving break, one of my leadership students, Jeanie, stepped into my office visibly bursting at the seams. Why didn't we fundraise for Lon and his family to help them through the Christmas holiday? It truly felt like a scene from a Hallmark holiday special. We planned it all and put forth the action within 24 hours. We never shared Lon's name with the classes, but instead told the choirs a member needed assistance. Titled Nickels and Dimes, a collection bucket epitomized a container of hope. When the staff discovered the project, they contributed warm clothing to Lon's family, whose winter coats still remained in storage from their last location. We collected enough money to buy Christmas dinner for the family and one gift for each person to celebrate on Christmas morning. When the family didn't need to spend money on food and clothing, their ability to rent a small apartment made the Christmas movie plot line complete. By semester break, the family moved out of the shelter and celebrated a real Christmas gathering.

Fast forward two years. Lon's work ethic produced great results in school. His singing voice gained confidence, which demonstrated the reason for his membership in the top two choirs and singing solos. Unfortunately Lon started to miss school. His family's only car, involved in an accident, made a trip to the shop never to return. Since Lon did not live in our district, school bus service did not exist. Completely reliant on students and me to transport him from his parents' downtown apartment to school, he still continued to miss days at a time.

I couldn't accept the possibility Lon could flunk out his senior year. The principal surely would provide a solution. I asked him if we could fundraise for Lon so he could at least take a taxi to school. To my surprise, my principal responded with "Let's just buy him a car!". He suggested we start a GoFundMe page. I felt the warmth of God's presence walking by my side. This school possessed the power to reach out to Lon and help him end his senior year with success.

The principal called in our bookkeeper for guidance. He also served as the school's compliance officer. The principal presented his idea to fundraise for a new car through a GoFundMe account. The bookkeeper agreed it was a great idea. The one stipulation: our school needed to remain anonymous on the GoFundMe site. I contacted Lon's mother and received the bank account information to funnel the funds. That evening I carefully set up the page and started it off with my own contribution. I saw it as a wonderful opportunity to invest in a student's future. Within days we attained close to $3000.00. Everything fell into place until the phone call, which would ultimately tip the scales to end my career.

Lon called me in tears. His grandmother just passed away in California. He and his mother wanted desperately to attend the funeral. May he possibly use the money from the GoFundMe account for airfare to attend his grandmother's funeral? Since the money from GoFundMe deposited automatically to Lon's mother's bank account, he did not need my permission to spend it. No other choice remained but to give him my blessing to use the money for the trip.

The next day in school, I shared with all my classes what happened with our anonymous choir member. With Lon's absence, his identity was not a secret, although no one spoke his name. Everyone felt so sad this young man could not catch a break. Several suggested we send around the bucket and collect money for Lon to make it through the holidays, which we did.

And thus began my two week nightmare. Lon literally disappeared off the face of the earth. He would not return my phone calls, text messages or email. Lon's vanishing appeared as if he "stole" the GoFundMe money and used it for an adventure. When he showed up after semester break, my anger seethed as I inquired his whereabouts. Why no effort to reach out to me? Did Lon even comprehend this whole episode held the potential to end my career? He shrugged his shoulders as a typical teenager, waving the red flag of defiance. This followed with attitude delivered in sulking silence. My anger heightened as I related the concern for my integrity. Lon abruptly left my office, on his way to the principal's office. Upon his return, Lon assured me the principal understood the money's use for the trip for his grandmother's funeral was legit. I thought the issue closed until Dave, my administrator, informed me about Mr. Jones.

Mike, the son of Mr. Jones, apparently decided to share his youthful interpretation regarding the Lon fiasco, with the assumption I misappropriated the funds. Mr. Jones, like some parents, must believe teachers imbeciles and thugs. As if things couldn't get worse, a second preposterous accusation: I graded his son in direct proportion to the amount of money his son gave to the GoFundMe drive. The entire conversation would seem almost laughable, for the exception this father's determination to ruin my reputation and ultimately end my career. The administration willingly transitioned as Mr. Jones' accomplices.

Dave informed Mr. Jones he was never apprised of my initiating the GoFundMe drive. (I researched my emails and found the GoFundMe information, which Dave received but must have strategically ignored.) Mr. Jones, celebrating the waning support for me, now possessed the ammunition he needed. He climbed the administrative ladder to my principal's door. The principal spun the conversation regarding the set up of the GoFundMe account as entirely my doing. My entrance under the front wheels of that proverbial bus moved quickly. When Mr. Jones could see no administrative support prevailed for my actions, he did what any entitled, arrogant parent loved to do: he drove a few miles to the superintendent's office.

The district requested I produce all paper work regarding the GoFundMe drive. I knew by this time in my career the expectations of those dotted i's and crossed t's explicitly. I provided the appropriate paperwork. The district never contacted me again regarding this fundraiser for Lon. No accusals of misappropriating funds. Yet Mr. Jones sent me a message via the superintendent's office, delivered to me by my principal. Mr. Jones retained an attorney and he would use him if I ever attempted to raise money again. My principal informed me I could no longer remain in charge of my many fundraising accounts, since he could not trust my decision making process. I followed all the rules for fundraising, deposits and withdrawals for eight years. In one instant, my track record and my good character counted for nothing.

The final nail in my coffin of dismissal hammered by duplicity of parent and administrator. Mr. Jones won, as well as the other four parents. Their entitlement mindset, unkind assessments and an administration determined to support the parent over the teacher ended an illustrious 46 year career. The hot rubber of the bus wheels created a stench which choked my very being. The innuendo of misusing money became the final statement on my virtual career headstone.

Teachable Moment: Do not fundraise for any one or thing in your classroom! It's that simple. No way exists to track who gave what. For decades I collected monies openly to aid world catastrophes, philanthropic organizations, and individuals in

78

need. Never once did anyone question me about the money raised. Ironically, the schools I taught in did school-wide fundraisers without any clear way to insure money collected contained a paper trail. Times changed, drastically. My fundraising for Lon placed me in a compromising situation, which never bodes well for any teacher under today's parental microscope.

Another Teachable Moment: How do you confront entitlement in your students and your parents? You cannot do it alone. If your principal feels afraid to support you, start looking for a new position. The lack of administrative backbone will only escalate parents' bad behaviors. The more parents believe thinly veiled, negative accusations will be accepted by the administration, teachers will become target practice for anyone who feels the need to complain and time to do so. Meetings behind closed doors, emails and phone calls will never solve or satisfy real or imagined problems. In order to find a solution, all parties involved need to gather in the room together to insure a productive outcome.

And Yet Another Teachable Moment: One of my most supportive principals handled parent complaints in this manner: to the parents he would say he held all confidence in me. He sought my interpretation of what happened before he assumed my guilt. How refreshing! If the parents took it further, he would defuse the situation without even including me. He retained that much faith in my ability to do my job. This principal, who understood entitled parents could skew perceptions, insured my 15 years at that school remained the best of my career.

Watch Your Own Six: Through the years, you may need to justify almost everything which transpires in your classroom. The following represents teaching practices to avoid the onslaught of undeserved criticism:

- Keep records for your records.
- Make sure those people who oversee financial transactions sign off on any district accounting procedures you use.
- State your classroom and grading policies publicly.
- Develop a website where you can post documents, calendars and information, and do so diligently.
- Answer all parent concerns within 24 hours. Use email to form a productive approach to document what questions came up and how you answered them. Keep the answers short and professional. Write your response as if it could be read at the school board meeting, because it just might.
- Keep all potentially controversial emails for at least two years. You will have a record of any unprofessional pattern of behavior.
- Discipline fairly and hold high expectations for your students. Do not allow a dissenting parent or the eventual involvement of an incompetent administrator discourage you from enforcing appropriate classroom norms and grading procedures.

If youth stared me in the mirror, I doubt my demise eminent. My administrator depended on my going away quietly due to my age. Never be afraid of the good fight. Join a reputable teacher's union or association if you believe your job to be in peril. On two occasions, I joined the organization when I felt unfair scrutiny from my administration. Having someone in the profession who listened to my issues afforded me a way to verbalize and problem solve my week to week conflicts with administration. Now do you understand that rescuing the teacher will save the child? Knowing what I do now, I would not have changed any path in my career! The Bible declares "Fear not!" 365 times. One walk in faith issued for everyday. I loved being a teacher. My faith insulated me from the troubled waters. Music still dances in my soul, although the fire doused by the disconsolate ending of my career.

The Not So Silent Majority: The majority of my parents, everywhere I taught, proved wonderful! But with anything in life, the negative far outweighs the positive. I could have 88 parents attend conferences and praise me. Two parents would question my ethics or philosophy. The challenge became remembering the 88 positive comments. I could always recall, verbatim, the two negative ones. Such is human nature.

My parent boards supported me through good times and challenging ones. Many came forward to express their frustration at my dismissal. Parents emailed me, but this time with incredibly heart-felt notes, about the impact music had on their children. The majority of my parents cared about me, wanted me to be successful for their child's sake and would fight for me if called upon. Hindsight being 20/20, perhaps I should have enlisted the aid of those silent majority.

Lest I receive blame for an unfair portrayal of parents, I am also a parent. When my son encountered rough patches in school, email was not available. I cannot honestly say I would have avoided using it when questioning his teachers. Writing notes and making calls seemed appropriate when seeking answers to my son's progress in school and in sports. Those communications never reached the acrimonious level of the ones I received.

Parents and teachers wear the same team jerseys! We both exist for the betterment of our children. Adversarial parents and dispassionate teachers have no place in today's educational system. Our children are too precious and their time in our schools too brief. Parents and teachers, when advocating for one another, could become the single positive force to change the course of our fractured public school system.

REFLECTION QUESTIONS:

STUDENT

1. Do you encourage your parents to complain on your behalf? If yes, what came of the results?
2. Did you witness your teacher in trouble after your "false claim?" If so, did you try to correct the situation?
3. When you faced a problem with a teacher, did you fabricate or embellish the teacher's actions in order to enlist the aid of your parents? If so, any regrets?
4. How involved should your parent get at the elementary level? Middle school? High school?

PARENT

1. Do you defend teachers when speaking about them in front of your child?
2. How involved should you get at the elementary level? Middle school? High school?
3. Do you take your concerns to the teacher first or to his administrator?
4. Did you ever complain to an administrator about a teacher, only to realize your complaint might have been unjustified? Did you try to correct it?

TEACHER

1. What philosophy do you maintain in dealing with parental complaints?
2. What actions should an administrator take when dealing with complaints?
3. How do you deal with a completely irrational complaint that has no foundation?
4. Do you hold fear of parental reprisals, so you acquiesce to their demands?

ADMINISTRATOR

1. What philosophy do you maintain in supporting your teachers regarding parental complaints?
2. Do you take time to fact find or do you assume the student and/or parent correct in their assessment of the teacher's performance?
3. Do you insist that students and their parents address the teacher first before you become involved?
4. Do you hold fear of parental reprisal which may render you incapable of protecting your teachers?

CHAPTER 6: TEACHING 1.1

"Show yourself in all respects to be a model of good works, and in your teaching show integrity, dignity," Titus 2:7

Out of the Closet: Parents beware! The chaos your child may cause in the classroom is very real! The math class embarked on its usual slow start. Mr. Peterson, a quiet and unassertive teacher, began taking roll. As his monotone voice drifted in the air, no one seemed to care. Simultaneously, a 15 year old girl, whose maturity manifested at 9 years old, took charge of the class with her frivolity. Entertaining the troops, at the expense of dear old Mr. Peterson, was due to Mr. Peterson's inability to squelch the behavior. Could a valid reason exist for this girl's antics? Yes! This child, and many children like her, saved their inappropriate behavior for school to escape the turbulence and strictness of home life.

Adopted as a baby to parents who never grasped unconditional love, she floundered through early childhood. These upper social stratosphere parents reminded her how lucky she should feel to live under their roof. Harsh reprimands, unreasonable punishments and physical beatings filled her earliest memories. She lived in constant emotional turmoil, never quite good enough for her parents' approval. By the age of 15, eliciting laughter from her peers presented the only joy in a disconnected life. This adolescent's hijinks would throw into disarray any teacher ill-equipped to control a classroom. The girl used this as an escape from the reality of a childhood filled with sadness. Unfortunately, her overactive sense of humor garnered approval from her peers, which only fed her insatiable appetite to amuse. This day, as with so many before, would present Mr. Peterson with its usual challenge of maintaining his classroom decorum.

He asked her nicely, several times, to "settle down." Her co-conspirators, while not openly participating in her foolishness, snickered at her boisterous behavior. This young punk of a girl manipulated the classroom to her fancy, unconsciously thriving on disrupting any academic work.

Mr. Peterson became more frustrated. His voice hinted of an oncoming reprimand, yet the authority statement faded in misguided attempts. The gentle man, who just wanted to instruct a math concept, tried in vain to proceed. But his red face belied his false sense of composure. The 15-year old continued to destroy his plans for completing the assignment in a timely manner. Engaged in her antics, she did not sense Mr. Peterson's close proximity as he startled her in the midst of her capers. He gently placed his hands on her arms and quietly said, "Come with me." The girl immediately enjoyed the new attention she reaped from her giggling peers. With Mr. Peterson's hands gently guiding her, she arose from her seat as he led the way to his coat closet. How hilarious! The students celebrated the scene, now with unabashed laughter. The young girl, in the height of her element, played to her adoring audience. Mr. Peterson calmly opened the coat closet door, escorted the girl into the 4' x 4' closet and closed the door behind him. He calmly said, "You can come out when you are ready to learn."

The darkness obscured everything in front of her, with the exception of a thin line of light between the door and the wall. The class quieted down, with not even a chuckle as Mr. Peterson began his instruction. How desperate the act of closeting her so he could teach? Why would it take this kind of episode for the young girl to finally stop and question her actions?

I do not remember the remainder of the class, as I stood humbly in the pitch-black closet. I wish from that day forward, I altered my foolish ways, became an outstanding student and experienced success because of it. I did not. But I started to make a gradual change, which would not see fruition until my adulthood. My grades stayed above average in high school, and only a little better in college. The excuse of my parents' hurtful home life determined my inability to succeed in school. I eventually made a metamorphic change from a lazy, entitled 15 year old to a productive and successful master teacher. Setting classroom parameters came naturally when working with children who found it difficult to reconcile the discipline of learning. I related well to those rambunctious kids, as they mirrored my childhood behavior. Their inappropriate conduct always reflected symptoms of something more serious, perhaps relating to their home life. A life lesson I knew too well. At the age of 15, I desperately needed teachers' intolerance of my actions and ineptness in preparing my school work. What I received, for the most part, were teachers who tolerated my unhinged conduct. They glanced at the clock, probably thanking God that only 20 minutes remained of my silly behavior. I believe the same may be said about today's classrooms.

Placing today's rude child in a coat closet would prove disastrous for job security, and rightfully so. Whereas many of today's inexperienced teachers would never contemplate the coat closet as a form of discipline, these teachers do contribute to their own frustrations when they allow poor behavior to take place in the learning environment. Ignoring a disruptive child and allowing him to manipulate the classroom cloisters him away from achieving, as well as prohibiting the educational growth of the other students.

The One and Only Rule: When I began teaching decades ago, I started with five rules:

1. Be on time.
2. No gum.
3. Try not to miss class.
4. Do not speak unless you have permission.
5. No harsh words.

I assured my students those rules were not only for them but for me as well. Eventually the five rules were replaced over time with 10 rules:

1. Gum free.
2. Seated by the bell.
3. Restroom before/after class.
4. Good posture.
5. Listen well.
6. Kind speaking.
7. Think positive.
8. Come to class.
9. Learn much.
10. Expect respect.

No need to copy those words for future use in a classroom. One and only one rule exists: Respect. In my classroom I permanently pasted the word **RESPECT** on my front wall. As I conducted my choirs, this concept could be seen at all times. The term had duel purposes: remind students that all behavior is set in the foundation of respect; remind me that if I did not mirror the word respect, I would not receive it.

It's All about That Pace: Early in my teaching I realized an internal clock moved me. When the lesson started to take a turn toward boredom, I intuitively knew it was time to change things up. Intuitively became the operative word. Teachers need a keen instinct when students' attention spans begin to wane. The younger the child, the smaller the teaching time frame of retention. In my naiveté, I thought I could teach pacing to student teachers. I soon realized pace was a skill instinctively based and not necessarily teachable.

Finding men who demonstrate real interest in teaching, especially at the elementary level, proves essential to the sustained identity of a male authority figure. When Arlan was assigned as my student teacher, encouraging him to remain in teaching emerged as my primary goal. According to the National Center for Fathering, more than 20 million children live in a home without the physical presence of a father. That does not take into account where fathers remain physically present, but emotionally absent. Men like Arlan were desperately needed in the classroom. But at what cost?

I did not have my own classroom and therefore travelled from room to room with all of my teaching apparatus on a three level cart. I began to perceive Arlan may not be up to the task. Five minutes to travel between rooms proved a challenge each day. Walking backwards, at least 10 feet in front of Arlan, I confirmed those elements which worked in the previous class. His snail-like stroll, however, impeded our arriving on time for the next class. Arlan appeared in good physical condition, but his internal clock seemed defunct. When I addressed this issue with him, he became defensive. Unfortunately, his lack of pace revealed itself in his teaching style. He could not control the 20-minute setting of a typical elementary music class. The children roamed around the room, completely disengaged with his teaching.

On Arlan's final evaluation, I suggested teaching might not be his forte. The outcome? A district hired him as a teacher upon his graduation. Perhaps his male gender earned him the position. I do not know if he stayed in teaching. Hopefully he worked with a mentor, making the transition to a capable instructor. This procedure of sending out unskilled student teachers to become educators remains apparent today. Over the years, I watched twenty-something teachers unable to facilitate a simple lesson plan. Their inability to perceive pacing added to their null and void classroom management.

Teachable Moment: If you have the privilege of taking on the role of cooperating teacher, make sure you also have the power of assessment of the student teacher. There should be a clear rubric in order to pass on an individual into the teaching profession. While recruitment of talented male teachers should be a constant motivational force for any university education program, conveyor belt issuances of ineffectual educators must be discontinued.

Classroom Mismanagement: If you cannot manage your teaching time or classroom, your students will NOT experience success. In the 25 years I worked with student teachers, classroom management seemed missing from the curriculum of pre-student teachers. But how could classroom supervision not be the topic du jour? Many university professors never ventured into the public school K-12 system. These pedagogical geniuses of subject matter avoided the concepts of K-12 classroom management. They never found the need to implement it at the university level. If these higher learning educators did spend time in the public schools, the stint was short. These professors intuitively knew teaching in the ranks of post secondary education could warrant a better career. It should be no surprise many student teachers entered the classroom with not an inkling on how to quiet the students to begin the class. These future teachers learned to shout over the din of noise and accepted poor student outcomes as the norm. If you do not hold command of the classroom, organizing a hierarchy of learning skills becomes almost impossible. Constant interruptions by students, sounding like a clamor of indiscernible noise, became the usual fare. It did not take those adolescents long to perceive the person standing in front of them did not possess the finite skills to control the room.

Teachable Moment: The philosophy of Teachers' Colleges needs to become more relevant for today's educators. Possessing an excellent skill pedagogy will hold no benefit in the classroom if the instructor standing in front of the room cannot control the learning environment. I find it interesting when viewing the resumés of esteemed university education department faculty. Most have not spent much time in the reality of teaching K-12 in a public school setting.

In order to transition a student teacher into the classroom, I required the following:

1. Observation of my classroom procedures, instructional language, discipline and teaching practices was required before the student teacher could take the reins (two to four weeks).

2. Team teaching small segments of the lesson (three to five weeks) initiated as the next step.

3. Teaching without my presence in the room (last three to four weeks of the term) was the final skill set. My office was closed off, inside the rehearsal space. This allowed me to vacate the room without leaving the student teacher completely alone.

Even with the above plan, student teachers may go oft awry. I knew things were going poorly for one of my student teachers when the end of the term approached. I sat in my office, with the hopes she reached a point to teach without my interaction. A well-crafted paper airplane flew by my window, which affirmed this lovely student teacher lost control. I wish this situation only true for the student teacher. Unfortunately, I observed seasoned teachers unable to maintain order in their classes. An example is popular teacher, Miss Claremont. On a brightly colored sunshiny day, this social studies educator in her 10th year of teaching, allowed her students the enjoyment of experiencing class in the courtyard. It was challenging to detect her, dressed in her usual jeans and t-shirt, amongst her yelling and running high school students. She perched herself on a picnic table, looking intently at her computer, while her class used the courtyard as a running track. Ironically this teacher, deemed by the administration in the role as staff support for our classrooms, appeared detached from the day's instructions. No learning could possibly take place in this utter chaos. The students always suffered the most when their teachers disconnected, if even on one spring afternoon. The paradox about "popular teachers"? Students talked amongst themselves how they disliked a teacher's class where no order existed. They really didn't care if the teacher appeared cool or dressed like them. If they couldn't learn because of the discord, these students felt ready to bail.

What Is Assertive Discipline? A great answer to classroom management. When my son was little, Dr. Spock's voice transformed child rearing with a less authoritarian approach. But I attempted to raise him by my parents' standards, which sometimes showed harshness with no results. I needed to break the chain. My parents believed in corporal punishment. How could I stop using that approach with my child, yet make sure he understood consequences would come from his youthful poor decisions?

During a television talk show, I heard a discussion about assertive discipline. This new approach of making children accountable without spanking or irrelevant punishment solved the challenge of constant verbal battles. The basic concept evolved around stating (not asking) a reasonable change in behavior, with the expectation it would indeed change. The statement, followed by a consequence should the child disregard the request, reinforced him to accept the desired behavior. The operative words at the end of this sequence involved this phrase "it is now your choice." I stated calmly: "Clean up the toys and then you can play over at your friend's house or leave the toys and stay home. It is your choice." Voila! It was successful. Yes, times existed when his room looked to have experienced a tsunami. I needed to accept his choice with my consequences. Ultimately, with patience, he acquiesced to the request. This procedure didn't work when I found myself in a hurry or feeling tired. The same holds true in teaching. I would catch myself stating these nonsensical phrases, especially when exasperated: Do it because I said so. My way or the highway. I don't care what you think, I'm done dealing with you. How many times do I have to ask you? Or my favorite: I've told you a thousand times to stop talking. If I told a student to do something 1000 times and he chose disobedience, changing the tactic was on me, not the student..

The following comes from *Assertive Discipline* by Lee Canter:

1. Develop a teacher voice: say what you mean and mean what you say.
2. Give constant and clear expectations throughout the class period: do not ask for students to do the work but instead expect them to do it.

3. Give expectations at the beginning of each semester, both verbal and written. Having a class syllabi for older students is a necessity. (I published a class handbook and syllabi on my website which proved a great way to insure a consistent answer to procedures.)

4. Give clear and quick consequences: use the operative words "you have a choice." (Example: "Please stop talking, Jan." She continued to finish her sentence. As soon as I began teaching, she turned and whispered to her friend again. When I asked her a second time to stop talking, she denied the whispering. Instead of getting into the argument tango, I would simply state, "Jan, please stop talking and do the work I have planned for today. Or you may continue talking, away from the class and makeup the work after school. It is your choice.")

5. Develop positive strategies. (We teachers do not respond well to surprise attacks, negative accusations or public admonishment. The same is true regarding our students. The Golden Rule [treat students as you would want to be treated] should always remain at the center of your classroom management. A case of a negative strategy: The English teacher assigned an elaborate project. When the dedicated student proceeded at great lengths to turn in the completed work, the teacher deducted 50% of the grade because the student did not include his name on the project. And we wonder why our children sometimes hate school?)

Teachable Moment: Many new educators and even some veterans avoid disciplining students or providing thoughtful instruction in order to achieve favored teacher status. Refrain from these aspirations! One of my professors dressed in a brown polyester leisure suit and had a pocket liner in his tan shirt. This teacher's clothing demonstrated all of the characteristics of what could become a boring summer school class. But when he conducted the seminar, he spoke with confidence, conveyed creative ideas, expected students to participate at a high level and encouraged us to have fun while we learned. It turned out to be one of the best classes I ever experienced in post secondary education. His method proved irresistible in wanting to achieve. By the end of that semester, the instructor dressed as a geek, turned out to be the coolest professor ever!

Consequences: The Ugly "C" Word: "If you get out of your seat one more time, without permission, you and I are going to have a problem. I just told you, do not get out of your seat while I am teaching. Did you not hear me? I believe this the third time I asked you to sit down." This conversation rears it's appalling head daily, if not hourly, in many classrooms. The above conversation could have gone like this: Adam, why are you continually getting out of your seat? (There may be a real issue you need to deal with, so knowing the reason the child is not sitting is important. When Adam tries to explain his antsy ways, listen.) Then reply it is difficult to maintain the classes' focus when he walks around. Perhaps he should sit over to the side of the class and then make up any missed work after school. It is now his choice. You haven't yelled at him, given him an unreasonable consequence or enabled him to continue his negative behavior. Assertive discipline worked well on those students who could rationalize. The perpetually angry student, who suffered from significant emotional problems, would need to be approached in a different manner. Usually those students maintained a plan where all teachers applied consequences the same way. If poor behavior became chronic, I needed to hand out consequences quickly and consistently. Through many experiments, the following provided the most success.

Three Warnings: On the first warning, a check mark placed in the grade book. No consequence, but instead a private conversation would take place with the student before he left the classroom.

If a second warning became necessary, the student would be required to meet with me privately outside of class time. At this meeting a questionnaire would be presented which could be answered with a verbal response or in writing:

1. Describe the behavior which brought you here.
2. How can I help you?
3. What is your plan for correcting the behavior?
4. Do you understand what the consequences will be if you should continue to experience problems? That questionnaire would be signed and dated by both the student and me.

Upon the third warning, the student would be temporarily removed from class if the behavior began impeding the progress of the class. If the actions appeared less grievous, the student would once again meet with me after school. The parent would be called about the continuing misbehavior, with the student present during the call. Further consequences would be discussed, with which the parent could support. This course of action took time, effort and patience. If you cannot commit yourself enough to follow through on negative behaviors, including staying after school, you may be in for a long haul. If you ignore the poor behavior, constant arguing and netting poor results from your students will become the norm.

If I took the time to follow my own steps, only one or two students per year received a third warning. Building rapport and traditions of high expectations with your students takes time, perhaps as much as two years. Do not become discouraged after only a few attempts of assertive discipline. Become the consummate teacher in classroom management and success follows hand in hand.

In one of my positions, I never used any warning system or consequences the first year. The high school students, mature for their age group, exemplified great self-discipline in the rehearsal period. I completed 11 years as a collegiate professor of music, so transitioning into high school classes where students demonstrated eagerness to learn held much pleasure.

However as each year passed, I noticed a lack of focus becoming more evident. The warning system was implemented and it showed signs of viability. I explained the system carefully at the beginning of each semester and published it online as well. Proof of the system's effectiveness showed through the lack of sudden blow-ups between teacher and student.

Why the change in classroom behavior? The middle school feeder programs did not consistently teach rehearsal discipline. I am an avid supporter of the feeder school program. That advocacy began when I taught junior high (grades 7-9). The two high schools my students fed into affirmed my program almost weekly, either by phone or by email. The high school directors realized their choirs could not sustain growth or integrity unless the feeder junior highs provided exemplary students. I needed to keep my end of the bargain and ready my students for the high school experience. The discipline of rehearsal would be an asset to any high school program.

One school's choir program philosophy was to teach their middle schoolers to love singing. No reading skills developed, but the children populated the middle school choir program to capacity. The other feeder school taught some reading and also gained success in recruiting students. Two other feeder schools contained high teacher turnover, so it proved challenging to discern what philosophy of teaching prevailed at any given time. Most of the middle school singers loved their directors, and of course my program benefited from that passion. However, two of those instructors missed one important component: discipline in their rehearsals. I would observe rehearsals in those schools only to watch kids moving around the room, talking to other students, not opening their music, and remaining completely disengaged to the lesson taught. When the directors, all excellent musicians, would speak, a constant babble of noise prevailed. Those wonderful singers, while having a fun filled casual rehearsal, never consistently received the discipline of the rehearsal. I implemented stronger consequences to offset the incoming singers from those two schools. Thus came "Take Five".

Take Five: Freshmen through seniors, who spent three years in middle school choral programs where the expectation to be quiet during the rehearsal did not exist, now populated my choral program. Keeping records on those misbehaving students became labor intensive.

Today's students hold much more aptness to challenge a consequence than the students I taught two to three decades ago. I blame the present political climate, reality shows, sitcoms and movies where students watch adults challenge authority on a regular basis, with complete disrespect and no consequences. Confronting a student in a public setting usually did not bode well. Not only could the student become belligerent, but his peers lined up right behind him, in complete support.

Kristy talked incessantly. She possessed a sparkle in her eye and a beguiling smile. This teenager boasted a phenomenal voice and stage presence. Her ability to entertain measured far above her peers. In my lengthy experience, I noticed students who emoted natural energy on stage could also have classroom issues with inappropriate behavior. I empathized with her personality wiring as she emulated my worst days as a young student of singing.

Her conduct, while not mean spirited, managed to find ways to take the rehearsal off focus almost daily. Her peers held her as their champion, which made the disciplining even more challenging. Students, unconsciously, will allow a popular person to ruin the rehearsal. But someone not well liked could not receive the same pass. How would I curtail her behavior and not lose her from my program? In preparation for the fall term, I needed to develop a plan where neither Kristy nor I would lose face.

At the beginning of the fall semester, I announced to all my classes if they could not dedicate themselves to the rehearsal, then they impeded it. No gray area existed. The implementation of Take Five became the new norm. Laminated 4x6"cards stated: *Take Five! You have a choice of going to the restroom, stretching in the hallway or going to the practice room to refocus. If you do not return in five minutes, you will lose credit for the entire class period.*

Students appreciated this method instead of arguing and confrontations. The card presented a graceful way of recovering. My student assistant kept a record in each class to whom passes were distributed. If it happened more than two times in a semester, I would conference with the child. On that fateful day when I visited with Kristy after her second Take Five, she confided the ramification of sitting in a practice room and experiencing remorse for missing the rehearsal affected her in a surprisingly poignant manner. Her senior year demonstrated a marked change in her demeanor. Kristy transitioned from a student demanding attention through thoughtless acts to a leader who demanded others in the class commit more fully. Her unexpected and wonderful change made Music dance inside me and rejoice. My fire burned brightly. And so did Kristy's.

Teachable Moment: To my delight, students initiated requesting Take Five. They exhibited proactive desire to avoid having issues. It proved the Golden Ticket. Even the worst case scenario positively transformed when handing out a Take Five and not having an argument or angry retort. My daily instruction became stress free and students appreciated the time not being spent on disciplining their peers. Interestingly, seldom did students take advantage of leaving the classroom. Our choirs received state and regional recognition so rehearsals held serious weight and the outcome rewarding when the class accomplished the difficult section of music with everyone in the room. Students realized if they missed out on rehearsing, when it came to testing them over the learned music, their grasp of the music would seem lacking. In a choir, the weakest link is a constant prevailing factor in acquiring success.

Off to the Office: Sending students to the office or a dean of students postponed the consequences which must be implemented by the instructor. Most importantly, do stipulations remain in place to assure the student actually arrived at the location when sent? The situation of a well-meaning admin refusing to discipline, but instead offering a sympathetic ear to a student pretending to be the victim of an unfair teacher, would not solve the behavior problem. Does any real fear of being sent to the office exist anymore? In my experience, the majority of admin earned little apprehension from the misbehaving students. Don't misunderstand the implications. They loved the admin person because he/she was "cool and chill." That demeanor is not helpful in the support of any teacher's classroom. I always felt it my duty to solve the behavior problem directly with my students.

Teachable Moment: Why should another adult be called upon to fix my problem? From the student's perspective, wouldn't that prove me incapable of handling the management of my classroom? The closest point between two objects remains the proverbial straight line. Deal directly with your students.

Behavior Referral: An easy procedure existed where I could enter a troublesome student's name into my data base's Behavioral Referral component. An explanation of what transpired, including dates and time, posted. The referral processed by the administrator assigned to that student's group. In theory, the student made an appearance in front of the administrator to discuss the behavior reported. Parents notified by mail. Consequences delivered. Theory and reality appeared to contradict each other.

Teachable Moment: The right to privacy appeared to be the pat answer when I needed to check on behavior referrals. Seldom did I hear anything from the administration or parent regarding the referral. It floated into an abyss, where matters of children misbehaving disappeared or simply remained ignored.

Classroom management, consequences for poor chronic behavior and follow through on those consequences ensured the best outcome from my students. The only times my classroom management broke down was when I felt physically and mentally drained. I would take the short cut and just scold. It held no effect on the student and made me even more exhausted by the end of the day. Good classroom management depended on my operating at my best.

Another Teachable Moment: I tried numerous ways of stopping negative behaviors in my classroom. All worked to some degree. But every year, when the personnel changed, I could not assume the previous year's consequences would hold the same affect on this year's kids. The way I managed my classes changed each year and sometimes with each new semester.

Documentation: My mind is far from a steel trap of events and outcomes. In the first few years of my teaching, my instant recall could provide a decent scenario when dealing with problems. It only took a few hazardous turns in my career to reinforce the idea of recording those actions, which might prove later a detriment to my forward progress. Documentation reinforced my memory and assured accuracy when presenting the facts. Undue scrutiny seemed palpable at times, which provided the motivation in preparing files chronicling the day to day obstacles.

Documentation is an unbiased, factual recorded evidence which recounts actions, reactions, time and date. When I first began documenting, the temptation to rebut accusations became challenging. However if I clearly laid out the facts of the situation, the reader should be able to come to the conclusion of what transpired without my bias.

If administrators questioned my teaching philosophy, it forced me to become adept at the written form. Those efforts gave an informal narrative about student, peer, administrative and parental behavior. I developed these methods over the years:

1. I color coded the passages in order to clearly separate facts from other references: Purple for Historical Reference; Red: Credibility Concerns; Blue: copies of emails; Green: reflection.
2. I dated (time, day, month, year) each entry of the document. It would be naive to believe next year might

possess a better outcome. Now I would have documentation of admin responses to show parallels from one year to the next.

3. Record the situation immediately, if possible. Any later than 24 hours, my facts became fuzzy.

4. Bullet the narrative and do not write complete sentences. Keep the documentation as brief as possible. Instead of rebutting, I added the green component "Reflection" at the end. The document would not become muddied by my defense mechanisms.

5. Emails always proved a great addition to record what transpired.

6. Documenting became therapeutic. When the day's trials compiled, journaling through documentation became a way to see clearly the events and in most cases, feel vindicated by how I responded.

7. Keep all documentation updated and on file.

8. Documentation did take time. On those hectic days, tempted to skip the detailed remarks, there appeared no reason to go through the effort. But experience taught me better.

180° In the Other Direction: Some teachers are just plain mean. We've all heard students say this, perhaps even your own child. Investigate the accusation, as your child's antenna may be receiving the correct data. Mrs. Smith taught English and believed firmly when the bell rang, her right to lock out late students took precedence. Anyone not in the room by the bell remained barred from participating for the entire class period. The work they missed could not be made up.

Mr. Clarkson required his science kids should always come equipped. If they did not have a pencil, they had to sit out for the class, make up the work missed and lose points.

Miss James would speak sarcastically to her social studies students. Her ridicule, demeaning and unkind rhetoric became famous throughout the school. Students came to my class after hers in tears, needing time to recover.

Countless stories existed of the punishment not fitting the crime or teachers making up new rules on the spot. They would veer off the grid with their expectations and with dogged determination refuse to change their ways. Their stubbornness prevailed until a parent reached out to the administration, handbook in hand.

The passive aggressive teacher demonstrates the worst characteristics of today's young educators. Mr. Johnson, one of the football coaches who taught history, mirrored this behavior almost daily. He vaguely stated expectations, used ridicule to prod students into submission, and then attacked them publicly if they did not follow his instructions. In the beginning of his tenure, he walked out of school at the end of the day with the students, never taking the time to meet with his students after school. When seasonal after school practices began, he refused to stay longer than two hours to help prepare the athletes. His teams proved marginal at best, yet the administration would palaver publicly about the skills this man possessed. He truly believed his activity held the only worth, thereby insisting his students be loyal to his program. When the athletes could not up the ante to support his expectations, he would state if they ever tried out again he would never put them on the team. A few parents tried to question his tactics. When Mr. Johnson refused to meet with them, the parents went to the administration. The principal did a lukewarm investigation of Mr. Johnson's favorite athletes and came to the conclusion Mr. Johnson had no issues. I never understood how those teachers/coaches kept their positions. I could only surmise it was largely due to being protected by administrators, who felt more comfortable being surrounded with inconsequential coaches and teachers.

Plans for Success: I taught 11 years at the collegiate level and never kept a record of my plans from the year previously. I held onto files of music used, to avoid repeats, but as far as concerts, community performances, staging and other musical ideas, no attempt to save became my norm. I wanted to change that scenario, so I began with small day to day plans which eventually evolved into yearly plans.

When I first started teaching, I wrote two days of plans in advance. That generated a lot of work, so I challenged myself with creating week long plans. It remained a living document, and I edited often. Designing strategies on a Sunday evening for the entire week proved itself much more efficient than making new plans every other day.

After my first year, I could see a pattern, so I developed monthly plans. Not intricate in nature, they instead gave me rough deadlines for repertoire to be completed, programs printed, reserving the auditorium, and communications sent out to parents. I found this quite successful, as it helped me to avoid being surprised and overwhelmed when the concert or contest season heated up. Thinking in the moment does not prove conducive to successful teaching practices.

My last discovery included the year overview plan. I did not begin work on this until my third year. Having the monthly dates proved a help, but sometimes I needed more than 30 days to prepare for an upcoming unit of study, concert or assessment. In order to run a multifaceted program, the lengthy plan looked incredibly complicated on paper. I began the fall term with all of the plans printed in red. As I accomplished each portion, I changed the font color to black. Periodically I looked back on my plans. If I found an assignment still in red, it motivated me to complete the action. It sounds like obsessive-compulsive disorder, but it worked!

Teachable Moment: Do what works for you, whether it seems obsessive-compulsive or not! Enlarging my yearly plans to reflect everything needed to maintain a forward momentum ended up a great way for me to anticipate what and when tasks required completion. I shared those plans with the administration, hoping they could visualize the amount of work required for a program to remain successful. The document, compiled of seven (single spaced) pages, covered everything from money due for fundraising, purchasing outfits for seven choirs and concert/contest preparation.

Assessing the Singer: Performing arts teachers do not always feel valued as a legitimate staff member. I've been called support, enrichment, elective, performing arts but never the simple term "staff" used to denote academic teachers. One parent remarked it was a shame I did not teach a "real subject" since I appeared to possess qualities of a master academic teacher.

Ever in the volatile position, I needed to justify my existence or be voted off the island. In my early years of teaching elementary music, the staff would debate, at the end of the year, whether they wanted to continue using precious points allocated for the music teacher. After all, they could hire four paraprofessionals in place of one music teacher. I reminded them my taking their classes for music helped accommodate their built-in planning time. Without me, how would they have time to meet with their colleagues and plan? Or have coffee? They would see the light and allocate the points to keep me. No one quite frankly cared if my students showed growth. I filled the role of the glorified babysitter.

In the 70's, schools began to look at the fine and performing arts as disposable subjects. The universities bear partial blame for the demise of performing arts programs in the public sector. While collegiate physical education and foreign language departments demand high schoolers enter post-secondary institutions with two years of physical education or a foreign language, the university performing arts departments did nothing to up the ante. There existed no requirement for any performing arts classes of graduating high school seniors. And again, no one cared if my singers showed growth.

In the early 2000's, one of the biggest fails I witnessed took place at a local university where music education was looked upon as unnecessary to the school's nationally acclaimed performing arts department. When my college students would audition for this neighboring university, the requirement entailed either performing opera literature or demonstrating high functioning ability with an instrument. My students, while possessing attributes of skilled singing, did not wish to pursue a performance career. These singers were sound musicians who held a passion to become music educators. As transferring community college juniors, their talent could not compete with their university counterparts. The university turned down these particular students in large numbers. When our college music department met with the local university professors, we discovered the music ed professors did not even receive invites to attend the auditions. This university wanted performers and not educators. I believe this true in many of our universities today. Music education is looked down upon, scoffed by professors who wish to live vicariously through their future performers and not their future teachers.

Presently, assessments of high school singers bear no weight on university music programs. Yet statewide measurement of student growth is required of most music educators employed at these high schools. So where does assessing the singer become a privilege and not a pain? If I wanted to legitimize my program, I needed to show proof something bigger than just singing transpired. In the 70's I began rigorously testing my students to show the direct correlation between reading music and reading words. One of my second grader's parent shared the following: his son came home disappointed he qualified for the lower reading group. But that disappointment found a broad smile forged on this young child's face when he proudly stated he could read music at a third grade level! Testing worked, and it brought greater buy in from not only administrators but also parents and students.

When I witnessed the increasing skills of my singers, I became even more resolved in my belief that assessing my students held importance for two reasons:

1. It showed administration I taught a correlation between reading and music
2. It motivated my students to demonstrate growth.

My resolve to assess my students increased through the years. In 2010, I submitted a paper to the Third Symposium on Assessment in Music Education entitled *Assessing the Singer: Making the Choir Accountable.* I received an invitation to present my paper to the symposium, held in Bremen, Germany that year.

The term "assessments" conveys light headedness, nausea and sweating to many educators. It became especially disheartening if teachers did not show growth in their students, they could lose their job. When was the last time we canned legislators after a term for not producing positive legislation during their tenure? Yet those same congressmen place so much pressure on today's teachers to prove their students show exponential growth. When the legislature passed a teacher assessment bill, many held concern over whether the ramification of the bill could allow a teacher to be fired based on the whims of his students' abilities to take national tests. People who knew nothing about education deemed it appropriate to place one more burden on their teachers.

The passage of this bill did not dishearten me, since assessments were already built into my curriculum. The first challenge was to find the component to assess, which would show growth. I chose sight reading, defined by vocally singing an unrehearsed eight measure example of melody/rhythm. If a singer could increase their skill at this activity, the following would take place:

1. Class time rehearsals proceeded much faster since the learning of the music became less labor intensive.
2. A sense of achievement encouraged the student to better his pre-test to his post-test score.
3. The level of music difficulty increased as students could comprehend the vocal line quickly and more efficiently.
4. I could demonstrate, with spreadsheets, the improvement of my students.
5. The program increased enrollment every year, despite the fact students knew they would undergo testing on reading music. Becoming a member of a choral program recognized as

ccompetitive provided status to those singers. The advanced sight reading enabled us to grow in both numbers and skills.

Teachable Moment: Fear of testing should not inhibit you from assessing your students. Find creative ways to assimilate the testing into your curriculum. Make sure you frame the testing to your students in a positive light. Hard spreadsheet numbers demonstrate the real progress. Some performing arts teachers chose recordings of their groups as one way to assess growth. To the non-musician administrator, the outcome would be challenging to evaluate. Many of my academic friends found assessments to be a positive way to encourage students to achieve at a higher level. If you approach testing as unfair and a burden, that will become the students' credo as well and there will be no turning back. I firmly believe that a teacher's evaluation should NEVER be based, even in part, on the success or lack thereof in his students' abilities to test. Taking this component out of evaluations will insure teachers do not feel compelled to "teach to the tests" or be punished due to students' lack of dedication in the classroom.

Assessing the Teacher: In chapter 7, I address the bias in teacher assessments with the Table of Comments section. It begged the question: how could a teacher demonstrate eight years of viable success, to be followed by the ninth year of a dismal performance? Administrators could make the assessment work for or against the teacher. The needless demise of Dr. Blevins, a high school math teacher, demonstrated the latter.

As new hires, Dr. Blevins and I suffered through training classes, IT threats and trees dying in the rain forest so the district could run reams of information on various colored paper. I was impressed someone with a doctoral degree would have an interest in teaching high school. Dr. Blevins, friendly and quiet in his comportment, seemed to be adjusting to the craziness in those few days before school started.

As the semester progressed, we "new" teachers were required to attend a lunch meeting once a week where we could share our experiences, receive new information about our departments and socialize. Everyone seemed to accept this time as necessary. Dr. Blevins, having taught many years, commiserated several times that seasoned staff were not exactly "new" teachers. Sometimes the meetings seemed redundant, held if only for the sake of scheduling a meeting. Nevertheless we reported with smiles on our faces.

One afternoon another teacher and I held a conversation in her office about how demanding and unreasonable one of the administrators behaved of late. Both of us received hostile emails, mine written in all red caps. Dr. Blevins joined us in an agitated state and asked if our conversation revolved around Don, the vice-principal. Since Don proved to be the topic, we asked Dr. Blevins why the frustration. He informed us Don was trying to fire him.

Two students in Dr. Blevins' math class took a strong disliking to him. The administration offered no support. As he continued his narrative, it became apparent plenty of teenage attitude dispersed itself onto this math teacher. Classroom problems need to be addressed immediately or they will escalate. One day after class, the students left a note on their desk declaring they were going to kill Dr. Blevins. Did this threat hold real merit, or simply a poorly thought out prank? With today's gun toting students, it was no wonder Dr. Blevins appeared paralyzed with fear. He asked for the two students to be removed from his class. They received two days of suspension. On the third day both students returned to his class, invigorated by no substantial consequence. The drama proceeded to the next level.

Don, Dr. Blevins' administrator, came to his class to observe. Dr. Blevins thought the class proceeded well and felt pleased with the outcome. When he signed off on the mid-year evaluation, he was horrified at the observation rating received. Don added things to the document which Dr. Blevins firmly believed did not actually transpire. Upon further reading, the evaluation made the good doctor look inept. This took place on the same day as the new teacher lunch meeting, where I was not in attendance. According to others, Dr. Blevins entered the conference room screaming, held his mid-year evaluation in one hand and began tearing it up with the other. He ranted about how unfair and despicable Don had been in this false narrative observation. The others in the room tried to comfort Dr. Blevins but his rage continued to build. Later that day he underwent removal from his classroom and I never saw him again.

I called Dr. Blevins and asked about his status. Due to his dismissal, he hired an attorney to fight the allegations. The entire fiasco of this man's short tenure saddened me. Instead of a belligerent environment of attacks, he should have been taken seriously when the students threatened his life. If he truly did not possess adequate teaching traits, then he should have been mentored. I saw the potential in this teacher. What if the administration took the time to initiate the three-pronged due process, addressed in the next chapter: identify the problem, give a timeline for the problem to be corrected and if not corrected, the consequence? The tool of observation must never be compromised or circumvented to reflect a false narrative. I would not have believed this could take place except the modus operandi felt very familiar as my EOY summary proved itself an exact replica of Dr. Blevins'.

Teachable Moment: Teachers may need to insist on the presence of video when they are observed. I cannot summon

111

in my mind why an administrator could feel empowered to doctor an evaluation but I witnessed it first hand. If teachers feel the potential of a false claim, they must become more proactive and assertive. This could include but not be limited to having a trusted colleague and an administrator collaborating on the evaluation.

A portion of teachers' assessments are student driven. Principals would hint some unhappy students complained, yet teachers seldom were allowed to converse with those students. Not knowing where the complaints came from led to a lot of frustration. A new study from Rowan University states a number of studies suggest student evaluations of teaching are unreliable due to various kinds of biases against instructors. The study affirms only a minimal correlation exists between student evaluations of teachers and learning: "the entire notion that we could measure a professor's teaching effectiveness by simple ways such as asking students to answer a few questions about their perceptions of their course experiences...seems unrealistic given well-established findings from cognitive sciences." In both my collegiate and high school teaching assessments, students' input was not only taken seriously but in Dr. Blevins and my case, used as ammunition for dismissal. At the age of 16, I shudder to think someone would use my anonymous remarks as a valid evaluation. Was I equipped to really understand what the curriculum would consist of and what the presentation should look like? Would I have the skills to know the difference between a dedicated teacher and a popular one? If a teacher made me work hard, would I necessarily find that a positive trait?

Another Teachable moment: Do not sign any evaluation or observation form unless you feel completely satisfied it accurately reflects your teaching practices. At my final meeting, my poor evaluation shoved across the table for me to sign, I hesitated on my next move. I sat in this gut wrenching meeting for 45 minutes where the principal informed me I would never return to my position. This followed by a demand for me to sign the EOY. I started to pick up the pen to sign, just to make this nightmare end. My union colleague stopped me, told me to take the evaluation with me, read it carefully and then sign it. The evaluation is filed away, some 10 months later and it still remains unsigned. It didn't make any difference to my demise, but it gave me a sense of satisfaction I refused to sign off on boldfaced lies.

REFLECTION QUESTIONS:

STUDENT
1. Do you make a purposeful decision to aid in your teachers' daily routines?
2. If you disrespect a teacher, why?
3. What characteristics do those teachers, whom you do respect, possess?
4. Have you considered becoming a teacher? If no, why not? If yes, why?

PARENT
1. Do you make a purposeful decision to aid in your child's teachers' daily routines? If yes, how do you accomplish this?
2. If you disrespect a teacher, why?
3. What characteristics do those teachers, whom you do respect, possess?
4. Have you considered becoming a teacher? If no, why not? If yes, why?

TEACHER
1. Do most of your students and parents try overtly to help you achieve success? If yes, in what ways?
2. Do you openly show disrespect for some of your colleagues?
3. What characteristics do those teachers whom you do respect possess?
4. Do you consider yourself a stepping stone teacher? a career teacher? What would make you want to leave this profession? What would make you want to stay?

ADMINISTRATOR
1. Do you make a purposeful decision to aid in your teachers' daily routines? If yes, how do you accomplish this?
2. If you disrespect a teacher, why?

3. What characteristics do those teachers, whom you do respect, possess?

4. Why did you leave teaching and become an administrator?

CHAPTER 7: ADMINISTRATING 1.1

Do nothing out of selfish ambition or vain conceit. Rather, in humility value others above yourselves, Philippians 2:3

Table of Comments: The human spirit, while somewhat resilient, will wither when beaten down by unreasonable expectations, falsified assessments, and total disrespect by those people in leadership positions. I witnessed my demise 425 days ago. My state of mind, although buoyed by colleagues, friends and family, seems reluctant to let go, move on or any other euphemisms inserted here. How could a teacher, who showed quantifiable success year after year, become the victim of such administrative contemptuousness?

Every year's end, teachers are given their performance feedback (End Of Year-EOY). I acquired nine years of those evaluations before summarily dismissed. I decided to do a direct comparison of years one through eight to my ninth and final year. Those eight years, all deemed successful, directly contradicted my final year. Our choir program attained the pinnacle of success, yet I received the lowest scores of my career.

Do not be naive. Administrators can and will alter a teacher's evaluation if they feel compelled to rid themselves of said teacher. In site based school systems, the principal has no checks or balances in teacher assessments. If you are a golden child, you will breeze through every year. Should you approach your golden years, the breeze turns to a cold head wind and blasts away everything you thought transparent and just. Such reflects my Table of Comments:

Administrator Comments Formal and Informal Written Assessments 2009-2016	Administrator Comments Actions, Formal and Informal Written Assessments 2016-17 **(Bold is a rebuttal)**
I'm going to end every week with a stop by your choir!	
You gave corrective feedback and encouragement.	
Paula is a master teacher of choir/music. She develops strong relationships with her students while holding them to high expectations.	Called into a meeting which lasted 55 minutes; administrator had a page and a half of typed notes he wanted to address regarding my poor decisions; told me this meeting was about him talking and me listening.
I love the way the kids support each other.	plays favorites with students and you're always asking them for money.
You did a check for understanding and discovered some confusion, which you fixed.	Some students ability to learn has been diminished

117

Administrator Comments Formal and Informal Written Assessments 2009-2016	Administrator Comments Actions, Formal and Informal Written Assessments 2016-17 **(Bold is a rebuttal)**
Your expectations are clear about classroom policies.	Student circulated a petition during my class seeking signatures on how I conducted auditions; when I took the document away from the student, I was scolded by this administrator for using class time to address the situation Administrator would not support my grading procedure when docking a student for only coming to 30 minutes of a 90 minute concert, which was clearly stated in the published choir handbook Both the district and I had policies directly dealing with student insubordination and grading; yet when those policies were implemented, the administration would not support my doing so
You helped students voice their opinions without putting down one another; all very respectful; great job of giving voice but still managed control!	plays favoritism and disregard student needs.

Administrator Comments Formal and Informal Written Assessments 2009-2016	Administrator Comments Actions, Formal and Informal Written Assessments 2016-17 **(Bold is a rebuttal)**
She strives to create a climate in which students understand the importance of maintaining respectful interactions within the classroom.	Brushes aside students' appropriate questions or concerns
She is very enthusiastic when teaching and this is contagious. Students pick up on this and demonstrate excitement and interest in learning.	Hinders the students' in their ability to improve and learn; **choirs recognized by the state governing activities body as some of the best in the state.**
Paula communicates regularly with students, parents and colleagues.	Ineffectively communicates with parents and student at the end of one meeting, administrator stated if I do not choose to heed those parent complaints, he may not chose to partner with me

119

Administrator Comments Formal and Informal Written Assessments 2009-2016	Administrator Comments Actions, Formal and Informal Written Assessments 2016-17 **(Bold is a rebuttal)**
Paula is a master of her content area. She has built a strong and popular choir program focused on learning skills.	There is a diminishing desire of students to continue on in music; **the program had just had auditions and all eight choirs filled.**
Paula does an excellent job integrating students with special needs into her classroom and into performances.	
Paula has developed a high achieving choir program and her students earn many accolades for their performances at competitions.	does not seek resources to build diversity in the community; **our choirs performed in a spiritual/ gospel concert where my students could choose to attend an African-American worship service; I used local musicians to play for our rock and country concerts; dedicated a semester to study the music of the Holocaust and used community members to help instruct; one concert raised $3000 to help the tsunami victims in Japan; outside resources helped us sell t-shirts to support the event.**

Administrator Comments Formal and Informal Written Assessments 2009-2016	Administrator Comments Actions, Formal and Informal Written Assessments 2016-17 **(Bold is a rebuttal)**
Her students are engaged and learning at high levels. Paula has a yearlong calendar that keeps her on track and addressing important issues.	Ineffectively communicates with parents and students
Students are positively and appropriately redirected when observed to be off-task.	attempts to respond to student misbehavior but with uneven results
Paula keeps accurate records and communicates effectively with parents and students.	financial records are not always in compliance with district regulations; **I was never contacted by the district with any concern about my records; on weekly discussions with the bookkeeper, she assured me that my record keeping was better than most**
While in class students are engaged in singing.	Hinders the students' in their ability to improve and learn

Administrator Comments Formal and Informal Written Assessments 2009-2016	Administrator Comments Actions, Formal and Informal Written Assessments 2016-17 **(Bold is a rebuttal)**
Friday medicine (is) watching you and your kids rock out.	
Your kids are working hard but also having a ball.	There is a diminishing desire of students to continue on in music
You keep their focus and sense of urgency up by setting tight time limits on each practice element.	attempts to respond to student misbehavior but with uneven results
Perfect combo of fun and discipline.	There is too much talking and not enough singing in choir;
A very positive and supportive teaching style is used to motivate students to give their best efforts.	We will be removing you from classes where money handling is a part of the course and where chances of negative student interaction can be minimized; **in other words resign or become a study hall teacher; this option had been offered before to two other staff**

Administrator Comments Formal and Informal Written Assessments 2009-2016	Administrator Comments Actions, Formal and Informal Written Assessments 2016-17 (Bold is a rebuttal)
	members who were being forced out
Your instructional style kept students motivated to do their best.	There is too much talking and not enough singing in choir; **yet these choirs earned some of the highest marks in competition both statewide and nationally**
a safe and productive learning environment has been established for all students.	Guests are not properly vetted; **my one teaching guest went through finger printing and vetting by the district; the other guests were former students who wished to consider teaching and wanted to observe my classes; when I asked if they needed to be finger printed and background checked, the response from admin came back as "no."**

Administrator Comments Formal and Informal Written Assessments 2009-2016	Administrator Comments Actions, Formal and Informal Written Assessments 2016-17 (Grey is a rebuttal)
You show genuine care and concern for all students on a daily basis.	insensitive to cultural norms
Your ability to make everyone feel comfortable and important is impressive.	There had been five parent complaints ranging from not putting a student into the talent show, changing how you auditioned students, how you graded and how you collected money for a student in need; I had previously answered all of these concerns in emails but now I am being grilled again as if we had not already had the conversations
Your knowledge of subject matter is outstanding and greatly benefits your students and others in your department.	

Administrator Comments Formal and Informal Written Assessments 2009-2016	Administrator Comments Actions, Formal and Informal Written Assessments 2016-17 (Bold is a rebuttal)
Students were observed working hard and displaying passion for music due to your commitment to excellence on a daily basis	
You have done an outstanding job helping all of your students enjoy music at whatever level they are capable of.	
Your assistance and input on the character education site planning committee this year was outstanding.	The trust of the office staff and administration has in you has eroded; **the previous principal told me that the counselors lost faith in me; when I addressed this with all four of our counselors, they informed they never held a conversation with the principal about any concerns regarding my conduct**
Students were actively involved in the lesson. they were given meaningful feedback many times.	

Administrator Comments Formal and Informal Written Assessments 2009-2016	Administrator Comments Actions, Formal and Informal Written Assessments 2016-17 **(Bold is a rebuttal)**
Real life experiences and stories used in lesson to keep students interested.	limit your interactions with students to that of a teacher role versus a counseling or show producer role; yet **we are constantly being reminded that we teachers are the last defense between an at risk student and failure.**
High but realistic expectations are in place for all of your students.	
You are a great role model and provide quality instruction to your students. You are definitely making a difference in their lives.	Students have a minimal respect and struggle with positive and nurturing relationships.
Students are held to a high standard of maturity and cooperation.	
Mutual respect is evident at all times. Students appear to enjoy your class and teaching style.	

Administrator Comments Formal and Informal Written Assessments 2009-2016	Administrator Comments Actions, Formal and Informal Written Assessments 2016-17 **(Bold is a rebuttal)**
She communicates clear behavior and learning expectations with students. She consistently gives positive praise to students boosting their confidence in performing.	
It is evident that there is mutual respect between students and Paula.	
You have the ability to appropriately challenge students of all abilities and help them feel successful in their efforts.	
	At my EOY, the first thing I notice is my name is misspelled throughout the entire document (Baach instead of Baack); **in their hurry to change my EOY, I believe they forgot how to spell my name**

127

Administrator Comments Formal and Informal Written Assessments 2009-2016	Administrator Comments Actions, Formal and Informal Written Assessments 2016-17 **(Bold is a rebuttal)**
	When asked about a GoFundMe that the principal had encouraged me to start for a needy student, this administrator stated that there was no proof that I wasn't pocketing the money; **he also claimed he was not given the information about the fundraising when in reality I found the email CC'd to him.**
	When I pointed out that the current administrator was using the same language as the previous principal (who tried to drive me out), he stated that maybe the principal had a good reason to get rid of me.

MY QUESTIONS:

I built a choral program from three to eight choirs without any departmental or administrative support. How could I not be safe in my position? I experienced success as a teacher only to witness the administration simply did not care. I used to share with my impressionable student teachers: if you give life blood to teaching, you will only bleed to death. Unfortunately I did not heed my own advice. A previous administrator understood my dilemma as a performing arts teacher. He shared his epiphany: If kids didn't like me and no administrative support in place, my classes would die and I would be without a job. I appreciated his enlightenment and accolades for growing the choir program.

At the February 2017 auditions, I filled all eight choirs. Why did my April 2017 evaluation say students dropped? My administration wanted me removed. Tenured and success meant nothing. The admin would say anything to rid themselves of me. This transpired without any consequences to the administration. The district prided itself in site based management which meant the principal played "mayor" of his own town. No evidence of checks and balances by the district existed to insure teachers' ethical treatment. The principal could hire and fire with no questions raised about his motives. If I felt unfairly treated, I could file a formal grievance. The grievance system, designed to force the complaining teacher to grow weary waiting for a response, raised questions of integrity on the part of central district. Often those grievances sat on one administrator after another's desk for the full 30 days. When the grievance process stymied the teacher from extracting justice, it moved on to the next level with no recourse except for the teacher to wait. My principal took a disliking to me, retirement age loomed on the horizon and thus my 46 year career screamed to a grinding halt. Music withered and cried inside me, and my fire all but died out.

How could I receive the award for outstanding choral director from the community, only to hear the principal evaluate my teaching practices as substandard? Awards meant nothing. Several years previously, I received an educator award from the state. My former principal never announced it at any faculty meeting. When it came time to attend the dinner and presentation, she neglected to show up for the event. Instead she sent the athletic director, whom I barely knew. I stood out as the only honoree whose principal and superintendent did not choose to attend.

I wrote a paper on how to assess choirs. It was accepted by the International Committee of Music Educators and I was asked to come to Bremen, Germany to present it. When I shared this with my principal, her email reply consisted of one word "congrats." My honor didn't even warrant the full word. She never shared that information with the staff or district. When I later inquired of her of the availability of any financial aid I could receive to help with the cost of the trip, her reply back contained two words, "good luck." She possessed a small vocabulary. I stayed home.

Why would already answered questions continue to be used against me? Administrators hold a general MO: if they want to get rid of a tenured teacher, they conjure up unprofessional charges to insure it all looks legal on paper.

One semester, a colleague came to my office in tears. She finished her EOY meeting with the assistant principal and he placed her in the three to four category (four being high). However when the principal found out my colleague received high ratings, she lowered all of them. Surely this presented an unethical and perhaps even illegal action. The teacher sent a letter to the superintendent about this situation and never received a reply. I asked the teacher if she felt welcomed at our school. She immediately exclaimed "no!" I shared the pattern of unprofessional treatment with previous teachers under this administration. If she stayed, she would be fighting the same battle. Hired by a neighboring district within three weeks, she still remains happy (and healthier) there.

How could the complaints of five parents end my career? The word "distasteful" comes to mind to think parents possess this power. In reality, they do NOT. The administration served this power to them on a silver platter, which later would hold my head. The five complaints presented themselves in either vitriol, lengthy emails or long meetings.

Who would defend me? Surprisingly, the silent majority of my parents rose up in unity and made the administration take ownership to my announced demise. A group of parents and students contacted the local paper and implored a writer to share my story. It felt gratifying to read in print about my unfair treatment. Those parents lit up the principal's switchboard, demanding to know the reasons behind his actions. Parents related the principal's response to my dismissal. The principal's deception followed a familiar falsehood: Mrs. Baack, while being a good teacher, chose not to follow protocol. Students went in tears to the principal to seek justification of my removal. He gave them the same slant. One student said the principal actually managed to produce tears in his eyes while explaining my dismissal. It was all lies, spin and theatrics.

I joined the union when the previous principal made it her mission to drive me out. My union membership kept me out of her crosshairs. When I called the union about my dismissal, sympathetic responses resounded. But they seemed incapable to advise on what to do. I visited with a colleague who sued the district for being fired without cause and won. How could she afford the expenses of the suit? The cost of a union attorney, since he defended her on behalf of the union, amounted to zero. That information appeared unavailable at the time of my dismissal. Several colleagues battled their districts in the courts, which also seemed guilty of dragging out the process. Did I want to sue and continue to make appearances in attorney's offices or court rooms for the next three to four years?

Sharing experiences through this book hopefully will mentor and encourage teachers to become proactive. What is my dominating retirement purpose? Educate students, parents, teachers and administrators regarding the need to affect change of teacher treatment. Taxpayers must better vet candidates for school boards, which in turn must insure superintendent candidates possess good moral character. Instead, most of these boards serve as a rubber stamp in supporting any action taken by the superintendent or school administrations. These same taxpayers also need to make their boards and superintendents accountable for the misappropriation of funds earmarked towards defending the district from suits filed by teachers wrongfully fired. Insurance claims including attorney's fees, court costs, and months if not years of litigation end up costing the taxpayers hundreds of thousands of dollars yearly. Perhaps more.

Could an educator with 46 years of successful teaching be forced to retire without due process? Yes. Success or attaining tenure did not insure anything. My a cappella group made semifinals in an international competition. The group appeared on television after winning the quarterfinals in February. They traveled to Dallas, Texas for semifinals in March. My dismissal went into effect in April.

How could I finish out 30 days with my students after such a dismal report from my administrators? Embarrassed about my circumstances of removal, how could I explain to my students why I would not return in the fall? That fear kept me away from school for two days. Meanwhile rumors circulated I quit and would not return. The principal asked my colleague to take over the choir program should I not return. My colleague stood more than ready to the task. If you think you can't get replaced in a heartbeat, you stand sorely mistaken. You will formally meet my student Frank in the next chapter. He and his appointed minions had my back. My last days were filled with parties, hugs, notes and gifts from my students.

The final concert will remain a wonderful, vivid memory. I received the outstanding choral director award presented by our community musicians to a standing ovation. Those visiting the concert remarked how my students' performances impressed them. God whispered to those around me and encouraged them to shield my heart in that hurtful time. I survived those final days, even though filled with tremendous emotional pain. In my heart, Music faded to a faint pulse. The fire of teaching sputtered and all but died.

Why would a just God allow this to happen to me? I saved the most difficult question for last. All throughout my career, but particularly those past ten years, I often questioned God about His rationale in my life. Why would He bless me with skills to teach, a passion to succeed, unconditional love for my students and a great knowledge of pedagogy? And at the same time, allow my life to endure colleague confrontations, dismissive administrators, angry parents and sometimes hateful students?

As an adolescent Christian, temptation drew me toward the nonsensical idea God would reward me and my life would become better, if only I believed in Him. I desperately needed God's sustenance, but I encountered a God who appeared to move away from me instead. In my carefree existence, the reality proved I moved away from Him. Now in my wisdom honed in pain, when I encounter life's turmoil, I truly understand the only difference between me and the non-believer is I have faith God will grant me wisdom, the peace which surpasses all human understanding and the strength to endure whatever life chooses to give me. He accomplished all of that in my walk as a teacher. I feel His presence now more than any time in my life.

Theory Differs from Reality: When I began my career in the early 1970's, protecting teachers prevailed as a principal's main purpose. Early in my career, an elementary school vice-principal did not like my approach to teaching and said so in a public meeting. To my complete surprise, the principal turned to the vice-principal and said, "I am going to tell you exactly what the superintendent of schools said to me when I thought the basketball coach picked the wrong starters. Shut up!" Someone coming to my defense never happened before and I am sad to say, has seldom happened since. Administrators in the 20th century insured the integrity of their staffs. The reality of the 21st century demonstrates teachers in a constant line of fire.

In my early days as an elementary teacher, I encountered first hand a principal who caused major strife for her teachers and parents. I attended a work shop at her school and ended up using the nurse's bathroom. When I came out, that irascible principal waited for me only to lecture I used the wrong bathroom. So I knew first hand of her abrasive style of leading. The parents met, ready to rid themselves of this principal, and began to devise a plan. I do not know if this was a recognized procedure for removing a principal, but I can testify it worked.

Creating Change with Integrity: The parents developed a three-pronged proposal:

1. The principal needed to change how she dealt with students, teachers and parents.
2. This change must be completed by the end of the next school year.

3. If the principal demonstrated an inability to show growth, she would face termination.

Who served as judge and jury? The superintendent of schools and an admin team from the district took the role of mentorship. Assessments throughout the year reflected her lack of commitment to improve. At the end of the year, due to no significant change of behavior, she accepted termination from her position. Due process used to be a common tool implemented by the legal system, school districts and the corporate world: identify the negative traits, give a timeline for change and consequences should the change not take place. This should prove a valuable tool in all instances. It would certainly be better than the blindsided midmorning meetings, where admonishing teachers and threatening them with termination appeared as the norm. The Tuesday noon meeting became my scenario. The expectation I would feel healthy enough to go back and teach the remainder of my classes revealed a flawed approach. Or was it purposeful to only cause more grief? At my midyear evaluation, my principal and I discussed my teaching part time next year with my colleague picking up more classes. There was no communication I could be terminated. Ending anyone's career is challenging, but less so if a well documented method and face to face communication serves as the protocol.

Support Is an Action Verb: What should support from an administrator look like? Complaining faculty members or parents must be considered with the intent of resolving the issue. The complainant should feel their concern heard, and a fact-finding conversation with the accused teacher should ensue. Sucker-punch meetings never produce positive outcomes. My defense mechanisms climbed upward as the conversation spiraled downward, leaving no real gain of understanding by the end of the meeting.

There should be an order to filing a complaint. No principal should listen to concerns about a teacher if that teacher has not been approached first. If meeting with the teacher first would feel awkward, perhaps that should serve as a litmus test to the validity of the complaint. If a parent or colleague wants to avoid a public meeting with the teacher, finding that groove in the tongue to remain silent might be the best action. However, if the teacher failed to listen or respond to the complainant, then a face to face meeting should take place with all parties. Email or phone calls should never become substitutions for resolving important issues.

I taught under a previous principal who encouraged his faculty to alert him if they found themselves guilty of poor judgment. He did not want to be blindsided. Whenever I could sense an upset parent, I would let him know immediately. If the complaining party called him, he already knew about the situation and could respond. Why do administrators insist on not getting blindsided, yet use this tool to intimidate their teachers?

Unfortunately my philosophy of alerting the principal to any perceived issues backfired on me. I shared a few conversations with Dave throughout the year regarding concerns put forth by a handful of parents. Nothing came of the complaints and in fact, all were easily answered and resolved. Yet at my EOY, Dave alluded to those complaints, even though he would have never known about them if I hadn't given him a heads up. As my colleagues remind me, "If someone wants to get rid of you, they will find a way."

My former neighbor came to me concerned about a teacher in her child's school. One parent spoke unkindly about this teacher and because of that, more parents began to believe validity in the grumbling. My neighbor believed this teacher, while certainly not perfect, possessed effective teaching practices. The other parent's gossip mongering concerned her. I suggested she courageously support this teacher. She did and in doing so met hostility from the other parents. However, a great outcome came from this sequence of events.

The group of worried mothers set up a meeting with the vice-principal regarding this teacher's supposed ineptness. They would not go to the teacher directly because it would create an "awkward situation." When they met with the assistant principal, she declared this teacher had nine years of great teaching practices. If the parents felt dissatisfied with this teacher, they could always choose to move to another school. How refreshing! This did not happen in my district, but instead in a neighboring city known nationally for proving itself an award winning school district, with some of the nation's top teachers. Shielding teachers from parents who want to rain hurt would be a healthy policy for all administrators. If a teacher holds a proven track record for successful teaching, it should be the principal's obligation to provide a fierce defense of this teacher.

As a parent, I experienced the same story line. I felt unhappy with our son's high school choral teacher. Every Thursday during the spring, our son handed him an excuse to compete in a golf tournament on behalf of the school. The director refused to take the excuse. When our son placed it on the director's piano, the director ripped it up and said he would not excuse him from choir. I felt this action completely unreasonable, so I telephoned (before the time of email) the teacher and tried to speak to him as a friend and colleague. I asked him why he wouldn't accept my son's valid excuse from school. He sounded "sorry." He explained so many students gave him invalid excuses. A week later, unfortunately, the choral director once again tore up our son's excuse to compete.

My husband and I made an appointment with the principal. At the meeting, the principal listened and then made this incredible statement. "Have you seen how many trophies this choral director has won? He is a top notch director and you must realize that his artistic traits, while being on the side of unacceptable to you as a parent, are appreciated by this school." End of conversation. Did I agree with this kind of loyalty by the principal? No. Arguably it could be said the teacher needed definite discipline from the principal. He chose not to, and we chose to leave the school. As a teacher, reflecting back on this incident, I would have appreciated the same protection. To my knowledge, in 46 years of teaching, I do not believe any administrator went to those lengths to protect me. One principal, in a backhanded compliment, told a disgruntled parent that my main flaw was I cared too much about my students. When did that become a fault?

The choir director role involves making decisions, almost daily, about who would sing in what choir, who would sing a solo, who would make the talent show and who would receive leadership positions. Those decision-making situations do not appear in the academic side of education. I knew another choral director who told his students if they complained about him to the admin, he would kick them out of choir. Did I agree with that approach? Of course not, but I understood it. By taking this stance, he taught unscathed while many of us in the same field constantly fought to defend our every decision.

District Handbooks: Theory or Practice?

Public Concerns and Complaints

It is the intent of the district to foster open communications with the community. The district welcomes constructive criticism of the schools whenever it is motivated by a sincere desire to improve the quality of educational or management program of the district. The district has confidence in its professional staff, however and desires to support their actions, in order that they be free from unnecessary, spiteful or destructive criticism and complaint.

Unnecessary, spiteful, destructive complaints defined my last year of teaching. The words from the handbook, while great on paper, did not exist in practice. The handbook contained further consequences addressing a student's "refusal to obey a member of the school staff or any behavior that disrupted the classroom." When a student felt he possessed the right to circulate a petition regarding my teaching methods, during a rehearsal, my actions of taking the petition away from him and reprimanding him did not receive support from my administration. Yet the handbook guaranteed my protection from student insubordination.

Teachable Moment: A catastrophic shortage of teachers currently resides in this country. Pay disparity reflects only one aspect of this issue. Perspective teachers do not heed the calling when they hear horror stories of administrators coddling parents and students. Children are now victims, teachers are monsters and the parent is always right. Why would anyone want to get paid so little, work long hours and then feel like the sacrificial lamb? Yet I did survive these negative traits of teaching for decades and I still loved my job.

However, now is the time to change this mindset of administrators.

Styles of Leadership: The following contains short summations of some of the administrators I worked with throughout my career:

1. He hired the best, stood back and encouraged his staff at every turn.
2. She held onto rules (some unwritten) which must be obeyed. No gray area or compromise.
3. She encouraged her staff to meet her expectations. If some of the staff could not meet them, the administrator stood by their side and mentored them.
4. She sat by the front door and would not allow her staff to leave before 3:30 pm.
5. One principal's philosophy was the Performing Arts existed as a fluff curriculum. Those teachers simply acted as a support staff for the school. Their non-teaching expectations would include lunchroom duty, cleaning up the lunchroom tables, crosswalk assignments and other non-teaching requirements. He believed those assignments justified a performing arts program.
6. She scolded staff for reaching out to troubled students. Her philosophy: only a licensed psychologist should offer suggestions to students. Come to work, teach your subject, and then go home.
7. He hired these teachers, so he defended them even when it became challenging to do so.
8. She could not deal with any parent who raised an issue. In a panic, she told the teacher to fix things with the complainant.
9. Some of his teachers taught longer than he had been alive. He trusted and supported them.

10. He organized face to face meetings when disagreements arose with his staff, parents or students.
11. She openly declared she did not like some teachers, and for no reason. If she couldn't fire them legitimately, she encouraged her admin team to drive them out.
12. She stated if staff received a parent complaint and did not acquiesce to the complaint, she would not support the staff member.

Out of the 12 styles of leadership, only one-third manifested a positive approach. Does our educational system elevate those who are inept educators to enter into the realm of administrating? Does the norm demand our culture just accept poor administrators? Dereliction in eradicating abusive student behavior, lack of integrity, and the omission of affirming teachers whenever possible creates chaos for today's children. Does the responsibility for all of the chaos fall on the administrators? No. However, people in leadership positions should possess the qualities of fair and balanced decisions, patience, and mentorship. Putting it simply: principals avoid, at all costs, making parents unhappy. These men and women leading the education industry show adeptness in saying just the right thing to the right person, sacrificing anyone not in the room.

Follow Up and Own Up: The performance went incredibly well that night. Both of my choirs attained the highest ratings. As we headed back to the hotel around 11 pm, the enjoyment of hard work and ultimate success permeated the conversations. We gathered in the lobby to watch the performance videos and read the judges' comments. I felt so close to those kids. Whereas their performances on stage warranted high marks, their sometimes lack of focus in the classroom challenged me. But tonight, we were one.

The next morning, the kids loaded the bus in good spirits. We began our two hour trip back home. My cell phone rang midway, our tour agent on the other end. She spoke in rapid machine gun utterances, communicating the words "vandalism and the police being involved," which stopped me cold. Nine boys supposedly vandalized three rooms and the destruction warranted the involvement of police. Through my anger, a feeling of numbness crept over me as I felt these young men could not possess respect for me and perpetrate such a degenerate act.

I phoned ahead to the admin team and told them what happened. I asked them if they could stay and visit with the boys upon our arrival. Those young men needed immediate intervention and consequences to insure this behavior would never be accepted as "boys will be boys."

On the remainder of the ride home, I placed the boys in the front of the bus with me. They profusely apologized for their behavior. I really didn't care at that point. I listened to them whisper amongst themselves, very worried about what would happen. Would they be allowed to graduate in one month? Would they lose their privilege to attend prom in two weeks? What would their parents think?

We arrived at school and I walked the boys down to the vice-principal's office. She greeted them with an air of sincere disappointment. In the conversation, all the boys agreed they really messed up. The vice-principal delivered the consequence: the boys needed to write a letter of apology to the hotel and to the maid who cleaned up after them. Really? For leaving pictures of penises, sinks filled with coffee grounds and half eaten food, they just needed to write an apology? I didn't reveal my disappointment over the lack of bite in this method of discipline. It remained the vice-principal's right to decide. After the short meeting, while walking down the hallway, the boys couldn't believe they got off so easily. No prom missed, no walk of graduation denied, no parent would ever know of their actions.

Since the vice-principal told them she wanted to receive their letters on her desk by the middle of next week, I felt the case closed. The hotel never called the police since no actual damage to property existed. A mess created by garbage, coffee grounds and phallic symbols demonstrated a total lack of civility from these young men.

As the year closed, I asked one of the boys involved what end game his apology letter produced. He forgot to write the letter. In fact, most of the boys never bothered to do so. I felt devastated and angry at the lack of follow through by the vice-principal on the lame consequences. Those young men learned one lesson well: you can get by with poor behavior, mess up public property and someone will bail you out.

Teachable moment: I should have followed up with the vice-principal and made sure the letter writing campaign presented closure. Never rely on anyone else to deliver consequences for your students' detrimental behaviors. The admin proved not capable of follow through. I should have implemented my own disciplinary action: the boys and I would have driven back to the hotel the following Saturday, where they would have cleaned the rooms.

Effecting the Change: Poor leadership styles and the lack of student discipline by many administrators prove common in today's schools. Our staff responded to the district's online administrative evaluation with the truth that our admin team's failures far outweighed their successes. Yet nothing changed. After several years of those useless surveys, with no district response, the majority of staff simply ignored the admin appraisal.

So how can change occur? The district leaders put norms in place for dealing with parental complaints and how principals should protect their staff. The expectation by all staff should be the actual implementation of those norms on a daily basis. Teachers venting on how the "parent is always right syndrome" pervades social media. The teacher retains no recourse but to cower and kowtow to the parent's every whim. How does our culture return to the era where teaching holds a revered place in society and teachers deserve the utmost respect? School boards, superintendents and administrators must foster an environment where teachers do not feel afraid to come to work.

It begins with the philosophy of the school district, demonstrated through the actions of the superintendent and the school board. Are teachers valued assets? Do today's parents hold a mindset of entitlement? Are children capable of understanding the day to day operations of healthy learning environments? Teachers cannot be effective with a backdrop of a hostile work place. Parents, while an important input of valued appraisal, must never hold the power to dictate what teacher stays, subject delivery, or appropriate discipline. In turn, children must understand their role of learner and not adjudicator.

Advocating for the teacher must be the primary goal of any district. This concept alone would act as a desirable recruitment and retention plan for educators seeking stability in their positions. Attracting highly skilled, professional teachers would not hold the challenge that it does today if districts resolved to hire the best and then protect their assets from constant persecution. Principals, who do not gain the staunch backing of their superintendent or school board, will fold to the complaining parent every time. Superintendents need to become involved in all of their schools and reinforce with their principals and parents that they will protect their teachers' integrity. What of the renegade, poorly prepared teacher? Of course complaints must always be heard and validated. If teachable moments come into play to alter a teacher's behavior, those should happen with the attitude of an advocate and not of an adversary. Relatively average teachers will grow in their positions if their department chair, colleagues and administration look at them with potential and not disdain. There should be a policy of strength communicated by the superintendent: teachers will not get fired without due process! Mentorship will insure they become the best instructors possible. Contemplate all the preeminent educators who would remain in teaching under that philosophy! Refer to the three-pronged implementation of changing behaviors: Make a teacher aware of their lack in skills, give him a time period in which the skills needed to be upgraded. If the teacher could not change in the time period allotted, dismissal of the teacher would be appropriate. This practice disappeared from the educational system years ago and became replaced by the adversarial method, delivered without thought or merit.

Principals who blindside teachers with a rancorous meeting should lose their jobs. Even the worst instructor deserves to be treated with dignity. Do we not expect the same with our students? Should a teacher hastily call a private meeting with a student, scold him for 55 minutes, tell him he would no longer be supported and expect a good outcome? If we expect due process treatment of students, shouldn't we demand it for our teachers?

Teachable Moment: Why did I spend the time summarizing statements and actions of my administrators? A glossed-over narrative of my treatment would not hold the evidence of conviction for the grossly prejudiced administrators I encountered. The best advice I can give teachers is to remember they remain at the mercy of their principals. I held a close and productive relationship with my administrator. Yet when it came time to defend me, I became his liability. He easily dismissed me, the success of our choir program and my 46 year career. In a democracy, where checks and balances prevail, the same must be applied to the school systems. School boards and superintendents use site based management as a way to separate themselves from the day to day issues which arise in their schools. No principal should hold the power to harass or dismiss without due process, the superintendent's support and the school board's approval. We teachers need to affect change in our treatment. Today's educational system needs repairing. Shoving out proven teachers because of age or politics will continue to be problematic in fixing the fragmented school districts across this country if immediate change is not implemented.

REFLECTION QUESTIONS:

STUDENT
1. What characteristics should a great principal possess?
2. Have you encountered a negative situation with your principal? If yes, why was it negative?
3. Have you experienced a positive encounter with your principal? If yes, why was it positive?
4. Do you feel your principal makes an effort to get to know the students in your school? If yes, how does he/she make that happen?

PARENT
1. What characteristics should a great principal possess?
2. Did you encounter a negative situation with any principals? If yes, what proved negative?
3. Did you experience a positive encounter with any principals? If yes, what proved positive?
4. Do you feel your principal makes an effort to get to know parents? If yes, how does he/she make that happen?

TEACHER
1. What characteristics should a great principal possess?
2. Did you encounter a negative situation with any principals? If yes, what proved negative?
3. Did you experience a positive encounter with any principals? If yes, what proved positive?
4. Do you feel your principal makes an effort to get to know you? If yes, how does he/she make that happen?

ADMINISTRATOR
1. What are your best assets? Where do you need to improve?
2. As a student, did you encounter a negative situation with any principals? If yes, what proved negative?
3. As a student, did you experience a positive encounter with any principals? If yes, what proved positive?

4. Do you make an effort to know your students? Your parents? Your teachers? If yes, how do you accomplish this task?

CHAPTER 8: LIFE LESSONS

Checkbooks, Clocks and The Calling: In 1971, I received the printout of my first teacher's salary and celebrated the feat of attaining yearly pay of $10,000. As my first year progressed, I analyzed the math concerning before and after school contact with my students. My teaching life consisted of evening concerts, weekend activities, lesson preparations and student assessments. As a new teacher, what was my first life lesson? I would never feel satisfied in this vocation comparing my checkbook to clock hours. The title of teacher proved itself over time as a sanctified calling, one not defined by salary or status.

A former student graduated from college with his bachelor's degree and landed his first job in the business world. In his exuberance, he shared his starting salary. While I praised his success, the realization his salary equaled my own (with two earned degrees plus 30 years experience) unearthed a startling revelation. Disparity in teacher pay proves shameful considering teachers are the frontline for the assimilation of our children into adulthood. The length of a day for an elementary child averages roughly 12-14 hours. During the school year, these young minds spend half of those hours sitting in front of an educator, ready to absorb all knowledge imparted. Children's social skills, ideas about the world, and scientific thinking all formulate in the classroom. Do we truly believe paying a teacher $58,000 per year (national average) seems fair in today's technology driven market of six figures?

Parochial school salaries are even worse. When a close friend shared she held two degrees and 20 plus years of experience but her salary averaged several thousand dollars less than mine, I was chagrinned to think I deserved better pay. She dedicated long hours to her work, captivated children with her creative crafts and through her dedication, her students read at a higher grade level. Where did fairness come into play? When I encouraged her to self-advocate for a better salary, she reminded me teaching was her calling.

In 1971, the "called" vocation made perfect sense emotionally, but not realistically in 2019. Where else, other than the teaching profession, does our society expect salaried individuals to work long stints without a break, arrive early and stay late helping students, supervise activities on weekends, fundraise to support beleaguered programs, prepare lesson plans and grade papers outside the paid contract? When teachers are paid six figures and professional athletes look to support their income with another job, teaching will once again personify the noble profession of decades ago.

What encouraged me to remain in teaching for all those years? The experiences working with incredible human beings who loved to make music proved quite enlightening. God called me to become a teacher and gifted me with skills for which I cannot take credit. My pay was never commensurate with the expectations of administrators or parents. I needed to move beyond the reality my business friends would always make three and four times more in salary.

God journeyed with me throughout my career. He lingered alongside me when I witnessed the baptism of one of my high school students. God's peace enveloped a former student as she confided in me she was raped by her brother's friend, while her brother watched. God's wisdom prevailed when I empathized with teenage moms and encouraged them to stay in our program as long as they could. And God's whisper that my assignment as a teacher to never judge my students, but only to love them unconditionally, felt most profound of all. That charge did not come without challenges. One of my former students was arrested for a smash and grab. I received his first phone call from jail, apologizing for the disappointment he caused and asking for assurance he could return to our choir program. The justice system disciplined him for his poor decision. He returned to singing and became one of our strongest leaders. In the words of my favorite composer, Eric Whitacre: "I don't know if it is a spiritual, physiological or psychological phenomenon, but I believe now more than ever that singing is a universal, built-in mechanism designed to cultivate empathy and compassion." And so Music smiled at my student and embraced his climb to success.

Teachable Moment: Celebrate those small victories you accomplished in the classroom and personally with your students. Perhaps a journal of those events could reflect how you intervened and changed the life of a child for the better. There are many in the business world who leave their positions to become teachers so they can witness real purpose in their lives.

Summers Off Misnomer: One mistake non-teaching professionals make is reminding us teachers we have the summers off. That statement alone could raise the blood pressure of anyone in the teaching profession. The moment school concluded, I spent my summers perusing new music, ordering music, cataloging it at school, cleaning my room, organizing concerts, contests and school year trips. I took one to two weeks of actual vacation in the summer. Teacher pay revolves around a 10 month salary, dispersed over 12 months.

Most of June, all of July and half of August are "unpaid" days. During that time, teachers prepare for the onslaught of the coming year for no remuneration.

As far as student vacations during the year, I truly wish they didn't occur! It always takes approximately one to two months to get students into the mindset of focusing on classroom expectations, and then they take a designated break. Once back from the break, the following week wreaks havoc of backtracking and reminding students of the classroom protocol. Multiply this by the weeks of vacations given students during the school year, and it becomes a wonder these young minds can actually retain anything.

The parent implemented weeklong vacations in the middle of the term frustrated me even more. Kids were given a week off for Thanksgiving break, and two weeks off for winter break. Yet some parents felt a need to take an additional week's vacation. A child not there during a week of instruction definitely impacted the other children. When the vacationing (often with a golden tan) child returned, catching him up and not stopping the forward progress of the others tested the abilities of any educator. Taking a child out of school for a week or more for recreational fun modeled that school did not take precedence. The practice devalued and de-prioritized the teacher's ability to instruct in a timely manner.

The same expectation must also hold true for the teacher. No valid excuse existed for me to schedule a recreational, weeklong trip during the school year. I discovered with my short term professional leave days that no matter the aptitude of the substitute, learning sometimes ended up on hold until my return. Some of the unproductive students, who loved to test the sanity of the visiting sub, negatively impacted the learning cycle.

Teachable Moment: Between full time positions, I worked as a substitute. All teachers should be required to sub before they become tenured. Only through this experience would they come to better appreciate subs, providing them adequate planning and rules for classroom management. Many times minimal sub plans lay before me. This forced me to think on my feet, maintain classroom decorum and still try to accomplish learning goals established by the missing teacher. I loved the challenge of subbing for one year. But when the year came to an end, I felt quite happy never to return to subbing again.

Good Plans Make for Good Subs: Throughout my career, I was blessed with dedicated substitutes. Commitment to provide a positive environment for my substitutes became foremost in my mind. As a substitute, I pretended to possess the power of the universe to instill learning, could call on anyone by name within the first 10 minutes of class, stated my expectations and followed through immediately with any needed consequences. I brought in my own supplemental plans to insure the class period progressed without issues. The following represents good teaching practices when planning for a sub:

1. Give plans for each class, with every minute accountable: no sitting around and visiting.
2. Stay away from movies. It is harder for a sub to maintain control in a dark room with the potential of students sneaking out or making out!
3. Have two to three students in every class who are dependable and will reach out to the sub if things go awry.
4. Get your directions laminated and in plain sight for any electronics used.

5. Let your colleagues know you will be absent and encourage them to look in on the sub.

6. Make sure your sub knows teachers are in close proximity, and they can help answer any questions.

7. Do not ask a sub to teach a new concept unless there is no way to avoid it. Write concise directions about expectations and consequences. If the sub can use the same language and consequences in class as you, he will be much more successful

8. In private, share with your sub any potentially serious problems. A phone call stating two kids in the same class participated in a verbal confrontation the day before demonstrates proactive planning.

9. Encourage the sub to give you feedback on how the session progressed and any insight they might have on the components of the skills reinforced. It is not the sub's job to discipline your students.

10. Make sure you follow up on any classroom issues described by the sub as non-cooperative behavior.

The Lesson of the Turtle: Taking on the challenges of subbing came with risks. Living a full and healthy life involves risk taking. Viewing it as a positive human attribute should be encouraged. Many years ago I saw a poster with a rather silly turtle on it, looking a little perplexed but nonetheless sticking his head far out of his shell. The words on the poster read, "To get anywhere in life, sometimes you have to stick your neck out." I loved that idea and decided to incorporate it into my elementary music classes. Seeing the correlation between taking risks and being a performer embodied my teaching goals. I encouraged my young children to sing out, loud and proud, as they shared their message of song.

When I moved into junior high, the lesson of the turtle became especially appreciated. My students loved the motivation to take risks. Soon weekly turtle awards provided further incentive for the students who best demonstrated sticking their necks out.

As a college professor, it was my Class Voice where I encountered a young lady who was terrified of singing. Each student was to prepare a solo by midterm. When it was her time to perform, she stood in front of the class of 25 singers paralyzed with fear. I suggested we turn the lights off so only the emergency light was on. This seemed to help but when she was in the middle of her performance, she ran out of the room. I found her in the hall crying and frightened.

The young lady decided to return to class. After the episode of not finishing her performance, she was resolved to make another attempt. This time she asked if the class would not look at her when she sang. We acquiesced, and she made it through the song. The time came for the final, and our young lady performed with the lights on and everyone in the room watching her! She completed the performance to a standing ovation, but not because she sang extraordinarily. She received the ovation because everyone in the room knew she achieved growth in the most profound way possible.

I ran out of the room after her performance, bringing back one of my display turtles from my office. I explained the lesson of the turtle. The singer's ability to stick her neck out embodied what every performer must experience at one time or another. With tears in her eyes (and in mine), she accepted the turtle. An awkward pause ensued, and I thought for sure my college students would roll their eyes out loud over such a silly gesture. To my surprise, the response chorus of "why don't you give all of us turtles after we have performed?" filled the room. From that day forward, the widely distributed turtle figurines symbolized the ability to overcome performance anxiety.

In the first year of my last position, while still trying to figure out the culture of the students, I received the task of overseeing an awards dinner for our singers. I followed the protocol of my predecessor and allowed the students to vote on each award. Then reality hit me. At the end of the awards ceremony, I found myself walking behind two of my senior girls. They had not received any award or acknowledgement. They gave four years to the choir program and walked out of the awards recognition empty handed. I vowed that would never happen again.

The following year, I followed the same protocol of the trophies awarded to a few of the voted upon seniors. The remaining singers received pewter turtles with the following poem, printed in color on a laminated flyer:

The Lesson of the Turtle
-Paula Baack

This little gift is just a mere toy
To help remind you, of the great joy
I have experienced in gathering with you,
Each rehearsal, our music to review.

I would ask you to remember this little turtle
And all the problems you will hurdle
When you continue to stick your neck out;
Challenging risks, some failures, no doubt!

The Native Americans from where I come
Sing of the turtles who do not run.
These turtles stop to enjoy earthly life,

Taking their time, embracing the strife.

But do not forget what others have said,
Each night before you retire to bed:
Stick your neck out, go after those dreams.
Soar to the moon and dance on the beams.

In the first couple of years, receiving a turtle with my poem did not feel the same as receiving a trophy. During those years some turtles found their final home under the auditorium seats, the poem crumpled up next to them. My third year, I held a conversation with one of my classes about whether they thought the turtle gesture seemed frivolous and should continue or not. One of my students stated her sister took her turtle to college. It stood on one of her shelves, reminding her to take risks. I decided to keep the turtle awards. Interestingly, I never found another abandoned turtle or poem. By the final year, winners of trophies inquired why they couldn't also receive a turtle. The small terrapin reaped great rewards.

Teachable Moment: My students needed tangible affirmation. Words meant something too, but an object to hold in their hand would last a lifetime. It went deeper than giving everyone a trophy. Making sure the students who committed themselves to our program received recognition became my primary goal. It promoted the longevity, loyalty and success of our program.

Walk in the Shoes of Your Students: Receiving recognition cast in a negative spotlight might seem less than a disastrous infraction, but understand your students' point of view. The usual buzz of auditorium noise reached a crescendo as we congregated for the first meeting of the day in a regional meeting of educators. I wasn't sure my colleagues from another state would attend. We hadn't conversed in two years so when I saw them enter the hall, I immediately stood and greeted them. We tried to catch up as quickly as possible, sensing the meeting would start soon. A few minutes later, over the blaring microphone, I heard this patronizing voice: If the three people standing in front would sit down, we could start the meeting. A hush followed, all eyes turned towards my friends and me. I could not conjure the remark directed at us. Seldom did anything embarrass me but I could feel my face warming with a faint glow. I, at 60 years old, had just been publicly scolded. Why would someone call me out in front of my colleagues in such a condescending way? Then the "ah ha" moment swept over me, like a cold wind. I sometimes shouted the same thing to two or three loitering kids when I opened my classes. The Bible states (1st Corinthians 13:12): "Now we see things imperfectly, like puzzling reflections in a mirror, but then we will see everything with perfect clarity." I never thought a verbal command directed at my students to be seated could produce an embarrassing effect. In a group of my peers, I disliked being chastised publicly. Perspective is everything. These are life lessons, which must be reinforced constantly to insure a teacher's positive interaction with his students.

How Close is Too Close: There are times when walking in those other shoes becomes complicated. One of my junior high students boldly stated she wanted to kill herself. I immediately took her to her counselor, only to find out this particular student used this approach to sucker teachers into feeling sorry for her. The counselor assured me I did the right thing about reporting. I felt embarrassed I couldn't see through the student's ruse. The counselor assured me I could not always take students at face value. But the best advice she gave me that day still stays with me: *I cannot save all my* *students.* Those resounding words came into play with Stephanie.

Stephanie sang in my junior high school choir program. She came across very personable and loved singing. Mysteriously, she would not show up for our required concerts. One day Stephanie confided in me her mother would lock her in her room every day at 6 p.m. so she couldn't go anywhere. I immediately went to Stephanie's counselor and Child Protective Services was informed. To say the outcome presented itself in a positive way and Stephanie went on to live a wonderful life would not be the case. At least, not at first.

From that point on, Stephanie was placed in nine foster homes over a period of six years (junior high through high school). I witnessed, first hand, the many issues with the foster care system. Stephanie would end up in a family with several foster children, little to no money and not much support. I watched her going downhill fast, feeling helpless and wishing I could do something. When I heard the "yellow flag" words from Stephanie, "I wish you were my mother" I knew it was too late to turn back. I became committed to this young lady's life pursuits, naive of the consequences.

Stephanie graduated from high school. Her counselor and I kept in communication throughout her high school experience, as I would try to be there for her as much as possible. Her counselor confided she felt sure Stephanie could never achieve much post high school. Fortunately for Stephanie, she did not heed those words. But a downward free fall would ensue before Stephanie would feel empowered to climb back up.

How close did our lives entwine? She would call in the middle of the night complaining about her collegiate experience out of state. Sleepily, I would crawl out of bed, go into the hall and whisper words of encouragement to her.

However, the words spoken held to no avail. Stephanie moved back, acquired an apartment in a questionable part of town and continued to live life in constant need. On a dark, sultry summer evening, Stephanie showed up in my driveway at 1 a.m. She sat in the passenger seat of her friend's car, hyperventilating and not making any sense.

In trying to prevent the hyperventilating from worsening, I could not find a small paper bag for Stephanie to breathe into. Instead I brought out a large grocery bag, which of course did not help with her anxiety nor mine. Stephanie gallantly tried to blow air into the massive bag as I contemplated what to do next. She refused to leave the car and now I grew concerned about my neighbors waking to this drama in our driveway. It never occurred to me that I could have avoided all of this by just letting go of this child when she left our school in ninth grade. I knew our lives were connected through divine providence. I left her with her friend as I went inside and called the police for help.

Approximately ten minutes later, a police officer literally stepped out of my bushes. Stephanie became so startled at the officer's entrance that her rapid pulse and short breaths escalated. The officer wrote down information as I tried to advocate for Stephanie. Thus far the responses to her situation only served to make things worse. Then the officer explained the mental health people would arrive shortly. Never think it couldn't get any worse!

It was 2 a.m. when a car parked a few feet from my driveway. A young woman, dressed in jeans and a t-shirt, approached Stephanie who still sat in the car. The mental health lady asked a question which even now remains challenging to process: "What is your name, and do you intend to commit suicide tonight?" This approach rocketed Stephanie into anxiety overload as she still breathed heavily into the large paper grocery bag. Done with patience at that point, I cautioned the mental health person her direct questions were not helping. She then informed me it was her first night on the job.

The police took Stephanie to the local hospital. They admitted her at 3 a.m. I did not see her for two weeks, as per protocol for the time period patients needed to recover and receive help. The hospital needed beds, so they dismissed Stephanie early. She continued to call me, seeking support and any help I could give. Only then did I realize I had become too close to the situation. I continued to enable Stephanie to postpone what she desperately needed: real treatment in a mental health facility. I didn't know what else to do, so I told Stephanie she needed to stop calling me. Two days later my family and I left for summer vacation. As we headed toward the mountains, Stephanie slit her wrists and swallowed a bottle of aspirin. She was serious about ending her life, but thankfully she did not succeed.

I did not find out about Stephanie's condition until I returned home a week later. I rode on an emotional roller coaster, feeling devastated and helpless. Due to the very real attempt at taking her life, a prominent mental health hospital in the neighboring city admitted Stephanie right away. I felt relief but also guilt for not being there for her. *"You cannot save them all"* became words which haunted me.

With Stephanie's release six months later, we reconnected. I carefully made sure she understood I could no longer serve as her emotional support system. She shared with me the six months in the mental health facility proved life saving. She finally opened up to professionals about her abuse at home, and how she suffered even further abuse in the foster care system. She also talked about her constant struggle post high school. I could see a new light in her eyes which gave me hope for her future. While at the hospital, Stephanie's doctor asked her to nanny her young baby full time. When Stephanie received the intrinsic trust of her doctor, her life turned to new possibilities.

Stephanie took care of her doctor's child for five years while she achieved something no one thought possible. She graduated from the local university with a degree in psychology so she could help others who could end up traveling the same path she followed as an adolescent and teenager. Stephanie and I stayed in contact. She gave me much of the credit for her recovery. But I knew her intestinal fortitude helped save her. When I moved to another state, we drifted apart. The last I heard, a special school for troubled teens asked her to join their team as a psychologist.

Teachable Moment: Her story, success and ability to overcome a constantly negative environment stands out as remarkable. I celebrated her story with my students, who needed assurances they could survive high school. But I also constantly jogged my memory so as not to blur the lines with those students who misunderstood my short term support for a lifetime of being there for them.

Life Lessons Taught through Rehearsals: In jest, I described my job as teaching life with a little music on the side. Whereas we would spend serious time on the music, there were meaningful lessons which would transpire during rehearsals:

- *Point of View:* Someone would complain that the person next to him was singing out of tune. My response: please state we are having some issues with singing in tune ("we" being the operative word). Learning shuts down at the first signs of calling someone out publicly.

- *Weakest Link:* Singing in a choral setting explored daily, sometimes hourly the weakest link rule: if one person did not focus it affected the outcome of the rehearsal. This holds contrary to an academic class: if one person decided not to complete the math assignment, it did not impact on the rest of the class.

- *For the Good of the Whole:* Working as a large group, one primary goal existed: make music worthy of the composer's expectations. Our singers, for the sake of the greater good, needed to take the nuances of their own solo voice and shave the corners off so they could resonate with and enhance those voices around them.

- *Positive Atmosphere:* One negative comment impeded the forward progress. In my earlier days of teaching junior high, the class period started with a student lead positive quote, which was placed on the walls of our rehearsal room. The poster above my doors stated, "Through these doors enter positive thinking people."

- *It's All About Family:* Long after graduating from our choir program, students would post on social media how much they missed singing. The reoccurring theme stated we were a family and everyone felt welcomed.

- *Outcome Based:* A choral performance embodied "outcome based goals" better than most subject areas. We would set upon the literature, rehearse it, memorize and polish it over six to eight weeks. Then, in a matter of minutes, our learning was demonstrated on a stage in front of parents and friends. I jokingly would challenge my academic friends that their lives would be different if they had to parade their students on stage, after every quarter, to perform what they retained.

- *Tough Love:* I found myself investing the most in those students who seemed to need guidance and caused trouble in class, but I did so willingly. Witnessing their turn around had the most profound impact on me as an educator. The students I spent extra time with, compelling them to fall in line with the expectations, would try to stay connected for at least a few years post junior or senior high. In some cases, we connected over their lifetime. Such was the case of Sarah.

Never Underestimate the Spoken Word: Reflecting back to that magic time of teaching music to junior high singers, growing pains always persisted as I began to find my true philosophy of teaching. I ran the gamut: I'm Ok, You're Ok; I'm Ok and You Are Not Ok; Stern, Uncompromising Choral Director and the ever popular Slacker Friendly Let's All Be Friends mindset. Then I watched a 60 Minutes episode about Marva Collins. Fired for having too high expectations for her inner city black children, she decided to start her own school. When Ms. Collins worked with each child, she painted a verbal success story. "Do you know how smart you are, John? Did you realize you could solve that problem, Cicely? I know you will be successful!" Her program proved itself exemplary as her at risk kids went on to college, having studied advanced math, science and Shakespeare. I wanted to emulate her. She became my idol, my champion of good teaching practices, and my hero who encouraged at risk children to achieve.

Then I encountered Barbara Colorosa at a workshop given to all teachers in my district. When she finished the presentation, I could hardly wait to get back to the classroom. Her main precept revolved around the idea of treating your students how you would want to be treated. Her two hour session impacted my life forever. Two outstanding women educators equipped me to bring even more success to my students. I tried to apply what I learned to every student I encountered. The life lesson I learned from this next story did not come to fruition until some 25 years after the fact.

Small in stature seventh grader Sarah faced many problems. She would prove herself a handful in class. I always remained uncertain as to which Sarah would show up. She held a very short fuse and I often found a way to accidentally light it. Her MO consisted of becoming instantaneously angry, shouting the word "unfair" and stomping out of my double doors, disappearing for the remainder of the day.

As with all my challenging students, I found talking to them one to one netted great results. Using my newly gathered information shared by both Marva Collins and Barbara Colorosa, I knew I needed to find a place in Sarah's soul where she could not only find success but happiness as well. Both of those educators believed firmly in finding a child's aptitude, calling that aptitude to the child's attention, rewarding positive behavior and possessing an insurmountable supply of patience.

I asked Sarah to come to my office. I affirmed the things she did well: she loved to sing and had a great sense of humor when not in a rage. Sarah respected me to the best of her capability. We worked out a plan where she would receive a reward if she could master her anger for three days. It seemed to work in the short term. But then came that fateful day.

Sarah entered the room and elapsed into anger mode in less than 60 seconds. I do not remember the trigger. No more ideas came to me, as she manipulated the time from the other class members. Anyone who touts the sage advice not to allow other people to steal your joy has not taught in a classroom. Sarah assaulted my double doors, crashing them open with both hands. Then this dark voice came out of me, the one only available when my patience escaped. "The Voice" made approximately nine to ten appearances in my four plus decades of teaching. The low pitched threatening instrument of my soul called out, "Sarah, if you walk out that door, I am done trying to work with you." She froze between the two open doors. I followed it up with those choice intellectual words, "I mean it!" Sarah did not move. In one of those miracle moments, she turned back around, returned to her seat and continued to improve with her demeanor. Why do I recall this now?

I taught at a school which could be best described as a compilation of yellow flags: the schedule did not reinforce retentive learning, the department remained polarized by egos, and administrators came and went like drifting tumble weeds. The Polly-Anna in me always thought it would get better next year. If you feel it's a bad place to work, do not remain under the delusion it will get better!

At that time in my career, arguably I could be called a Master Teacher. My colleagues never treated me as such. I asked a fellow teacher, who befriended me, what I was doing wrong. He felt it resulted from the new kid on the block syndrome. It was my fourth year at this school. How much longer would I need to teach to rid myself of the new kid complex? My collection of yellow flags looked like a massive bouquet of daffodils. I needed to resign.

I planned to submit my letter to the principal on that Friday. Writing the resignation letter proved challenging, as I did not want to leave without stating the issues, but at the same time, burning bridges never felt productive either. I painstakingly took a couple of hours Thursday evening to write the letter. I checked my email and something incredulous occurred. I discovered an email from a young woman who said I saved her life. It was from Sarah. She and I had not held any sort of connection for over 20 years. She found my email through an internet search. Sarah headed a group of people working with and for people who suffered from Asperger's Syndrome. When I taught her in the 80's, little was known about the disorder. Sarah informed me she had been diagnosed with Asperger's and went about setting up a blog. She recently posted an article about how one teacher, Paula Baack, saved her life. I wish I could brag it came out of a true heroic gesture on my part. But it wouldn't be true. I simply told her I would not work with her any further if she continued out that door. The command to stop resonated with Sarah and in her words, it changed her life.

How does Sarah fit into my resigning? I wept as I read how she revered my actions. The episode at the door long remained faded in my memory. But when she reiterated the moment that saved her, I did recall it. I felt embarrassed over something so small affecting her in such a big way. After I recovered from the emotional overflow, I could not resign. There would be more Sarah's, and I could not quit now. I am a believer in God whispers. My faith, since childhood, remained my guiding force. That evening, in the privacy of my home office, I felt God's hand on my shoulder. Why would Sarah reach out to me the night before I intended to resign? How could two souls, whose paths stretched miles and years apart, reunite on the eve before I planned to leave teaching altogether? God used Sarah to draw me to attention. I needed to continue teaching. I tore up the resignation letter and decided I needed to remain with this school.

Teachable Moment: Never underestimate the spoken word. Ironically my high school journalism teacher told me I could not write and took me off any portion of the school paper or year book which required writing. Yet today I find an exhilarating passion in putting thoughts into the written word. But I did not learn that lesson well. I told one of my singers she might as well quit singing because she didn't have the talent to make up for her lack of work ethic. She went on to perform for Disney. Be careful of your words and actions! There will come a day where the actions you think of taking seem completely appropriate. And then something will happen: a sign, a suggestion, or a God Whisper. Mentally prepare yourself to change your mind and your direction. Do not let your route stay etched in concrete. Be still and take time to listen.

Never Underestimate the Human Spirit: I spent five more years at that school. I found many more "Sarah's" who I believed God knew in His divine wisdom needed a Paula Baack intervention. One of my dear boys tried to commit suicide. When he recovered, I was the only non-family allowed to visit him. He ended up singing in my top groups. One year our concert raised $3000 for the victims of the tsunami in Japan. Kids filled my office, either wanting to chat or needing to share a concern about the welfare of another student. The counselors appreciated me, since I would constantly alert them to potential problems. God knew my spirit sought fulfillment in making music. He also knew there existed kids who needed Mama Baack's words of wisdom, a broad shoulder to cry on or just simply someone to listen to them. Music rejoiced inside of my soul when I helped them, and my flame burned brighter.

Then Frank came into my life. He did not enter the usual way. I first met Frank's parents the spring before his arrival. They told me Frank was diagnosed with Asperger's and this made him quite the handful. They did not go into great detail except to say that he currently studied at a school for troubled boys. Frank demonstrated a passion for music and he was equally talented at piano. I felt a genuine excitement to meet this Frank. I knew he could achieve success his senior year in our choir program.

Frank came in a couple of months later to meet me. He exhibited a man-child like appearance. His 6' plus frame and physical maturity spoke to the man side. His exuberant speech, quick change of focus and topics, and contagious laugher led me to believe Frank remained child-like in his spontaneity. This young man knew what he wanted from life, held a passion bigger than his personality for music, and wanted to become a part of our choir program. Frank played the piano for me. He could play by ear and possessed an incredible ability to transport his emotion for music into his hands. Frank could sing either tenor or bass. He seemed a dream student. I had never encountered anyone like him. His parents, Frank and I agreed this high school and our choir program would fit his needs for his senior year.

As I visited more with Frank before and after school, he became comfortable in sharing with me. He told his parents at the age of 14 he was gay. Frank felt like his parents never accepted him as a gay man. Meanwhile he took medication for his Asperger's, which made his emotions take wild rides. He also shared he believed in Jesus Christ. I knew Frank's senior year would yield high success because God knew Frank's heart. He wanted him to find a place to grow and achieve peace in his life. I became his hero as I tried to provide for him as many musical experiences as possible. His schedule looked like he chose to major in choir! When the students learned he could also play piano accompaniments for their solos, they lined up to request he play for them. The students genuinely accepted Frank and loved him for his skills. It turned into a lovely semester of pure joy.

In February, Frank became emancipated from his parents. He landed downtown at a youth shelter. They were crowded so he slept on a mattress in the hallway. I knew this situation held the potential for a downward spiral, yet Frank kept his cheerfulness and dedication to the choir department. When I discovered he rode his bike from downtown to our school, I felt amazement yet worried constantly for his safety. When I could, I loaded Frank's bike into my car and drove him back to the shelter. I could not believe the perseverance and courage Frank possessed. His parents stayed in contact with me, warning the honeymoon would soon come to an end and Frank could implode at any time. One day Frank confided he chose to go off all of his meds and he felt alive for the first time. I anticipated he might relapse, which could have caused serious consequences. It never happened.

With the help of another teacher, we found him a home to live in. God placed his hand on Frank's shoulder and guided him to a lovely family. When it became challenging to make school events since this family lived out of town, Frank found a fellow singer whose mother opened her house for Frank to stay until he graduated in May. It felt so wonderful to see God's work in Frank. While his life took a turn for the better, my life took a turn for the worse.

Throughout the year, I faced difficulties with a new administrator. At our first private meeting, Dave scolded me for 55 minutes. The usual handful of parental complaints came in about how I chose soloists or directed the talent show. For almost 10 years, my decisions, teaching style and program continued to be questioned as if I were a first year teacher. Administrators opened their doors to unsupported student complaints and faculty rumors, which created an atmosphere of distrust. I tenured my resignation. Only this time I delivered it to the district office and to my principal since I felt sure I could not endure anymore blindsided attacks. My principal acted shocked and set up a meeting to ask me to stay in the position. But there presided an ominous pall. I could see my demise in slow motion. What I perceived to be sincerity in my principal, as he encouraged me to rescind the resignation, turned out to be misguided. Unfortunately, yellow flags that flew for almost 10 years now turned flaming red:

- Dave, the assistant principal and my assigned administrator, declared he could no longer "partner" with me. Ironically he never even acted as a partner but instead placed himself in an adversarial position when he refused to support me against petty parent complaints.
- When the first parental complaint came in September, Dave advocated for the parent. Thus began the yearlong pattern.
- I noticed something alarming: Dave used the same language, to the word, of my former principal, who placed me in her cross hairs when it came to my teaching practices.
- After doing some research, I found my former principal mentored Dave when he pursued his administrative license. I felt doomed since my former principal tried to make my life miserable for five years.
- I approached Dave about how his language mirrored the previous principal who behaved in such an unprofessional way. Dave's response: Well maybe she had good reason to get rid of you. Of course this was stated in a private meeting.

Relieved of my position on that fateful day, I left school feeling sucker punched. It took me two days mustering my courage to come back and face my students. The administration (past and present) historically made lives miserable for the teachers they did not want. Teachers only won their filed lawsuits if they possessed the stamina to fight the district, who appeared void of integrity and professional behavior. For the second time in five months, I resigned. I had battled previous administrators, department colleagues and parents for the good part of nine years with no one coming to my defense. I was done. Music stilled herself inside me and waited patiently for justice.

What about this "never underestimate the human spirit?" Frank became my knight in shining armor. I know now I would never have stayed at school for the 30 days remaining in my contract if Frank's sense of honor and encouragement hadn't prevailed. In contrast to my serving as his hero up to this moment in time, Frank became my hero and validated my existence as a teacher, by actions instead of words:

- He immediately set up a meeting with the principal to demand he rescind my dismissal.
- Frank and my parents created a group of advocates.
- On the day I returned to school, he met me in the parking lot to escort me lest the administration stop me from returning.
- Frank organized other students to protect me from the administration for the remainder of the week.
- When the administration would not budge on meeting with the organized parental group, Frank went to the local newspaper to report on what he described as a complete injustice.
- He met with the reporter, making sure the story was accurate. Frank told me daily, if not hourly, how the parent and student community supported me and we would get through this together.

Frank, in his innocence, believed justice would prevail. He thought any day administrators would arrive at the conclusion they made a mistake. We discussed how God knew each of our paths. He made sure those separate paths became one. My parents called the administration and complained about my treatment. A handful of teachers in the building braved the trip to my office to say how sorry they felt. But for the most part, to be seen consorting with me would not be a good career choice. I never would have dared to guess what an important role Frank would play at the very end of my career. I firmly believe God knew I faced a huge upcoming storm and would need someone to validate me as a teacher. I am eternally grateful for Frank.

Applications for my position came in, and three candidates selected. One of them was the part time director I hired to cover the extra load. He came back from the interview glowing. According to his assessment, the administration seemed very receptive and gave him the impression he definitely stood a strong chance of receiving the position. However, lying in wait for five years was a colleague who had tried to undermine me and our program. Two weeks after my position posted, my job fell into the lap of the one who had waited impatiently for me to retire or expire.

Step number one in my recovery statement: I admit now I held no power over my fate as an educator. Within two weeks my eight choirs whittled down to five. The non-auditioned choir, where our special needs kids felt comfortable, became a part of the large auditioned choir. As one great philosopher once said, "Oh well."

Frank moved up north after high school and has been gainfully employed. We try to visit over the phone at least once or twice a month. I am still amazed at his tenacity for self-preservation and survival. My life changed for the better, as the song goes, because of Frank.

Teachable Moment: I survived effective omission, firing and getting forced out of several positions where the choral program experienced nothing but success. Each time I discovered something better always awaited me. Marva Collins experienced the same thing. She showed resiliency. Marva found people to loan her money to start up a school, featured on national television. As a teacher, you could attend the school and watch her teach for the week. I longed to do so and only wish I chose to take advantage of that offer. Ms. Collins passed away in 2015. Do not hesitate when opportunity knocks. Playing "what if" later in life serves no purpose.

Know When to Hold 'Em, Know When to Fold 'Em: At certain times in my life, prudence dictated to take a step back and evaluate where I stood in the education profession. Did I feel respected by my colleagues? Did admin remain supportive and complimentary? Did parents mostly stay encouraging? Did I enjoy the learning relationships with my students? Did I feel excited about reporting to school every morning? Did the load loom so large I needed to work nights and weekends in order to finish planning? Did I seem able to maintain a satisfying relationship with my family? In the beginning of this book, I referred to my own five steps of recovery as an educator. Step number four (I gave serious consideration and reflection to the many positions I held in the past.) popped up as missing from my career. I felt too afraid to admit it was time to move on.

Know when it's time to hold 'em, and when it's time to fold 'em. I shared in the pleasure of working with a most outstanding math teacher. Not only did she captivate her students in class, but her command of the classroom allowed students to possess input and support one another in the learning process. Unfortunately, she came under tremendous scrutiny from her department and eventually the administration. In a typical morning meeting on a Friday, Sharon received a summons to the office and summarily chastised for speaking her mind at a department meeting. After the lecture, which ultimately brought her to tears, the admin team sent her back to teach the remainder of her classes. Sharon called me that night, and we made arrangements to meet the next day for lunch. Over tears of anger and frustration, she felt powerless and out of ideas on how to combat those attacks.

Bullying is not only a characteristic of indifferent children. An administrator demeaning a teacher into submission resembles the bullying of children by their peers. Through intimidation, administrators created an environment of hopelessness through unscheduled, blindsided attacks. Sharon received a veiled threat she might not be employed at the school the following year.

An opening came up at a neighboring high school, but Sharon felt reticent to apply, as she taught in her position at the high school for eight years. She garnered a great respect from students, parents and peers. But Sharon could now see the writing on the wall. She applied for the new position and was hired. Now thriving in an environment of affirmation, Sharon couldn't feel greater happiness. She only wished she had decided to make the move earlier.

Flashes of "what could have been " remain engraved in my heart. When I second guess the decision to remain at the last position for nine years, I feel conflicted. Instinctually I knew after the first three months on the job, the admin and department members did not operate with competency, integrity or empathy for one another. Staff morale could be determined as mixed to low when I arrived in 2008. That fall, 18 others walked by my side as new hires. By 2016, 17 had left. Yet, if I trust God's plan, I must concede that He did not error in my placement. I met hundreds of gifted singers, many of whom I was afforded great collaboration opportunities. If I knew the first year of my employment at this job would end my career in the most hurtful way, I might have reconsidered my tenure. Hindsight and reality should never find themselves in the same conversation. I loved growing the program to eight choirs and only sighed when I witnessed its collapse to five choirs two weeks after I left. Yes, Virginia, there is no perfect teaching position. And you can be replaced in a heartbeat.

Teachable Moment: I placed a post card size reminder on my home mirror which reads *Change Takes Courage*. While that message may seem simplistic, as a teacher you must recognize those jobs which should come to a close, if for no other reason than to preserve your physical, mental and emotional health.

REFLECTION QUESTIONS:

STUDENT
1. Have you been there for someone in need?
2. If you knew of a peer or teacher being falsely accused of something, would you possess the courage to stand up for him publicly?
3. Have you held a close professional relationship with a teacher? If yes, did it prove itself a positive experience?
4. What life lessons have you learned already?

PARENT
1. Have you been there for someone in need?
2. If you knew a teacher being falsely accused of something, would you possess the courage to stand up for him publicly?
3. In your days as a student, did you hold a close professional relationship with a teacher? If yes, did it prove itself a positive experience?
4. What life lessons would you share with your children?

TEACHER
1. Have you been there for someone in need?
2. If you knew a teacher, administrator or a student being falsely accused of something, would you possess the courage to stand up for him publicly?
3. In your days as a student, did you hold a close professional relationship with a teacher? If yes, did it prove itself a positive experience?
4. What life lessons have you learned already?

ADMINISTRATOR

1. Have you been there for someone in need?
2. If you knew a teacher or a student being falsely accused of something, would you possess the courage to stand up for him publicly?
3. In your days as a student, did you hold a close professional relationship with a teacher? If yes, did it prove itself a positive experience?
4. What life lessons have you learned already?

CHAPTER 9: MAKING THE COMMITMENT

I epitomized **Mrs. Holland's Opus**. In the movie, Mr. Holland's Opus, Richard Dreyfus played a band instructor who taught school as a stepping stone, waiting for his opportunity to compose music for a living. Spoiler alert: teaching actually proved itself his calling and dream job all along. His story resembled mine in the early years. I spoke these statements so many times:

1. Teaching is perfect because I'll have the summers off to be with my kids and for vacation.
2. I hope to become an actor, but in the meantime I'll teach to put food on the table.
3. The business world didn't fit me, so I decided to become a teacher.
4. I graduated college and just didn't know what to do, so I decided to try teaching.
5. My dream job of becoming a (fill in the blank) never transpired, so I decided to teach instead.

Number four resounded as my personal favorite. My journey as a college student dismantled before my eyes as I lost my motivation. In the early 70's, teaching seemed like a great solution, especially for women. I implemented my short term plan to retire after a few years and raise a family. The best laid plans go oft astray.

As a single parent, my vocation as a teacher remained the only way to support myself and my son. Elementary music education became the perfect fit. Teach young children to sing and then go home. Only two concerts per year, no state assessments, and elementary children possessed the power to make me continually smile. As a music educator at the middle school level, a choral director position prevailed as a bona fide job. Barbara Colorosa awoke that passion inside of me. She asked the assembled teachers of our district if any of us could display our own business card. Few hands with cards raised. Dr. Colorosa challenged us to think of teaching as an elevated profession and not just a stepping stone to something better. I ordered my business cards the following day.

In the 80's, my personal life took off in a positive direction. The support of my husband allowed me to whole heartedly commit to my job, teaching grades 7-9 choral music. The significant word "commitment" regulated my life.

Society must advocate for the positive treatment of teachers as they dedicate their lives to our children. Determined communities, in order to retain committed educators, must shield teachers from over encroaching parents, test driven evaluations and trepidatious administrators. A painfully real emotion, burnout can quickly manifest itself before a teacher realizes it. I experienced it the most when parents and/or administrators decided to place me in their crosshairs of criticism. A quote from Anatole France: *Nine-tenths of education is encouragement.* If that is true for our students, the certainty of truth holds firm for our educators. My seeds of passion and commitment always triumphed over the cynics. My students deserved the best from me, which in turn provided them with the best experiences possible.

Vigilance At All Times: Communities, school boards, administrators, teachers, parents, students and especially universities must remain vigilant to protect teachers from a hostile work environment. Doing daily battle with children and adults drains the soul to depletion. The national teachers' movement generated dialogue regarding pay disparity. Equally important, if not more so, a sincere exchange of resolutions should take place to ensure positive mental and physical health for our teachers.

Communities should make every effort to vet school board contenders to insure knowledge based educational values thus avoiding an agenda based on political influence. What constitutes their educational backgrounds? Did they teach in the public school system? Are they parents of school aged children?

School boards need to set expectations for their principals. Mentoring by administrators insures teachers will be able to achieve the best teaching practices. Students' test scores should reflect only a minuscule part of the total picture when assessing the teacher. Heavy reliance on those scores discouraged many educators from continuing in the field. School board members need to advocate against the use of such scores. If board members demonstrated the same pre-election exuberance after elected, perhaps these members could affect positive change in their districts. Do they possess resolve to insure teachers' freedom from vitriol criticism and frivolous complaint? How do they avoid, inadvertently, becoming a rubber stamp for ineffectual or bullying administrators?

Administrators should never have the option to fire a teacher without a due process document on record. The art of mentoring teachers has all but disappeared in the public schools. It has been replaced with acerbic dialogue, false accusations and retribution innuendo. Administrators should invest their own time in professional development to understand the true meaning of mentorship. Doctors enroll in bedside manner classes. Principals need to receive instruction on growing their teachers' confidence. The art of constructive criticism succumbed to abrasive and unfiltered attacks. Children are NOT victims, teachers are NOT monsters and the parent is NOT always right. Dereliction in eradicating abusive student behavior and the omission of shielding teachers from unwarranted condemnation wreak havoc for the teaching profession. Administrators should be required to deliver judicious faculty assessments, exhibit unbiased decisions and willingly provide guidance.

Teachers must view themselves as the whole body and not pigeon-holed into their room or subject area. If one staff member receives a volley of unkind remarks, stand together and support the person under fire. More than likely this pattern of unwarranted attacks will spread if unchecked.

The recent national teacher strikes addressed teacher salaries. Could a credible explanation of poor teacher salaries partially rest on the fact women dominate this workforce? In many cases they are secondary income earners for their families. Could that stymie the salary negotiation process? The presumption a teacher should feel compelled to work evenings and weekends in order to complete the curriculum sets forth as an unreasonable expectation. We women educators must be proactive in changing salaries, which better reflect teacher work hours. Teachers spend the most time with our impressionable children. Students exposed hourly to new ideas, philosophies and problem solving skills require the very best in our educators. Yet their teacher must attain a supplementary job in order to pay the bills.

Parents ought to walk in the shoes of teachers. Treat them as if your child's success depends on it, for it does. Writing incensed emails to your child's teacher and believing it is your right to submit such rancorous opinions is the most demoralizing act perpetrated on teachers. If you find it awkward to speak to the teacher face to face, re-evaluate the validity of your complaint. Your children are entitled to an equitable education. They are not guaranteed high grades, a lead in the play or varsity standing.

Students need to comprehend no teacher exists, including the ones they dismiss as inept, who doesn't feel the day to day rigors of insuring their success. Today's children need to avail themselves in committing sweat equity to the work required. Instead of complaining about instructors, challenge yourself to positively impact their daily routine.

Universities must commit themselves to a higher level of ownership with their future teachers. If candidates cannot demonstrate integrity, pedagogy and an aptitude for teaching, they should not be allowed to continue in the teaching field after their sophomore year. The hiring practices of post secondary institutions should be placed under scrutiny. Do collegiate faculty possess relevance when it comes to real world participation in a public school classroom? Or have our universities once again maintained the ivory tower syndrome where dissertations are plentiful, but true know-how of navigating K-12 public teaching experiences are null?

Recruitment is Not a Bad 'R' Word: Universities do not appear to do much recruiting of suitable teaching candidates. Perhaps these institutions could learn from the teacher in the trenches and how recruitment is a valuable tool.

As a performing arts teacher, my livelihood depended on recruiting students, retaining them and hoping they (and their parents) remained satisfied at all times. Looking back, I perceive recruitment as the most labor intensive of all commitments and probably the most diligent way to maintain a healthy program.

In most of my last 35 years of teaching middle school through college, I cannot recall a time where administrators or colleagues helped me in recruitment. In many cases I chased down the same students for my classes as my fine and other performing arts colleagues. The emphasis of loading middle and high school students' schedules with AP and honor classes translated into less room for electives. Although recruiting became an intensive aspect of my job, the success of my choral programs depended on it.

Although the academic teacher would find no need to recruit, the following might offer ideas in assimilating middle school children into the high school community. In order to sustain a choir program, I found these activities fostered the connection with our community and feeder schools:

- Recruited middle school kids to our program through voluntarily teaching classes at their school, judging their events, and inviting these kids to perform at our school.
- My choirs performed three programs per year at our feeder schools. I stayed and visited with students afterwards.
- Auditioned middle school students on site of their school. Incoming freshmen placed in auditioned, higher achieving choirs would insure their commitment to our program.
- Held planning sessions with the middle school choral directors. Developed goals and creative ideas to insure both programs benefited from each other.
- Created a website where students and parents could see, hear and experience our choir program.
- Our choirs collaborated with the feeder schools' choirs in joint public performances.
- Posted my audition procedure on our website, which included sound files to help students prepare for their audition.

Now proceed through the list and contemplate how university teacher programs could reach out to high schools in order to generate interest in their program. In my decades of teaching, I never experienced recruitment on that level. More importantly, I did not experience universities reaching out to teachers in the field to tap their resources, creative ideas or positive teaching practices. The only recruitment I witnessed was inviting teachers to come back to further their degrees, which involved them paying out tuition. I contacted several universities and colleges in my immediate area to see if they would be interested in my addressing today's educational issues with their student teacher program. I volunteered a gratis presentation. Most never responded. My experience is many of our higher institutions of learning appear detached from solving the issues facing educators today.

Commitment to the Uncommitted: Mick and Adam exhibited much talent as singers. They were afforded membership in a local choir, where the best from the city studied advanced choral repertoire. Their egos stroked in the city choir, the two young men appeared unhappy with our choral program and vocally deemed it unworthy of their talent. Yet they continued to sing with our high school groups. Within their second year, an adversarial relationship developed between the boys and me. They questioned my authority, which forced me to preview everything stated in class to avoid conflict. The other students dreaded the confrontational environment, which became the norm.

During this turbulent time, a summoning to the principal's office every six to eight weeks became commonplace. I witnessed trumped up accusations from unknown sources. Keeping my composure through those caustic meetings, I began entertaining doubts about my ability to teach. How could my principal articulate minor classroom issues and elevate them into dramatic teacher problems? From whom did she receive this inside accounting of daily rehearsals? Why was my integrity questioned at every turn?

Thank God for students who are endowed with character. Jackie asked for a time after school, where she could speak to me privately. We met in the quiet of my office. She stammered and looked down at the floor. As her voice broke and her eyes welled up with tears, she shared a colleague met with my students whenever I was absent from school. During those meetings, this teacher encouraged students to write letters to the principal regarding the supposed demise of the program. I felt shocked, hurt and betrayed someone manipulated my students with an agenda of terminating me. Jackie shared this colleague asked her to write a letter but she refused. She took a huge risk by warning me what transpired behind my back.

Over the next few days, my frustration, reflected in my classroom demeanor towards this deceitful colleague, grew more intense. Annie and Coral approached me after school and called me out on my poor behavior. They could not understand my lack of kindness when talking to this teacher in front of my students. Why did I change my teaching practices in just a matter of a few days? The girls and I maintained a wonderful working relationship, so I understood their disappointment with the pall I cast in every class. I decided to share Jackie's words of warning. The two girls looked at each other, gasped and then both started speaking at the same time. In their exasperated voices, it became clear this same colleague asked them to write letters as well. There could only be one hypothetical answer: a plan, perpetrated by this teacher, possessed ammunition for my removal. For the two years remaining, Annie and Coral protected my six. They explained to Mick and Adam, in rather base and explicit terms, their negative classroom attitudes would no longer be tolerated. The students' letter campaign ceased, so the principal perceived no justification to call me in for further tongue lashings. Our program and I survived, but reflecting back none of that behavior exhibited by the lying in wait colleague should have been allowed to happen, let alone continue for months. At the end of the year, the teacher who headed up the campaign to remove me, moved out of the department. How did I recover a broken program which underwent such unwarranted scrutiny? My desire to commit to my students translated into an even more substantial program, which replaced the need for retribution.

I decided to create a theme for the following fall. It was *I (HEART) Choir*. My leadership students and I met in the summer to devise a plan to heal our program. The students decided to come in and decorate the choir room before school started. Our rehearsal area became heart attacked! Hearts of every size pasted on walls or hung in doorways. The program lived to breathe another day.

The complainers no longer received fuel to place on their fire. The enrollment of our program increased, adding a new choir every other year. To my surprise, the students suggested another theme for the following year. Every year after that, the students selected the theme for the year and volunteered their time to decorate the room. Posters, positive sayings, and the display of our awards connected with students as they entered the room. We not only survived the crisis but the silver lining behind those clouds demonstrated students bought into the choral program at a greater level than ever before. In conjecture, perhaps those proactive students realized a few disingenuous students, manipulated by a staff member bent on destroying my reputation, almost cost them that program. Music rejoiced inside me and our singers. Our fire burned brighter, flames blazing.

Commitment to the uncommitted took yet another positive turn. One of my close friends, Trish, taught history at our school. She became visibly upset when I related what materialized with the colleague trying to negatively influence the choir students. Trish taught both Mick and Adam and initiated a meeting. She informed the boys about the plot to send me packing. According to Trish, the boys immediately voiced disgust towards the offending teacher and her manipulation of them. By the end of Mick's senior year, I received a hand written apology. One year later, almost to the day, Adam sent me a kindhearted letter in the mail. I will never forget how they reached out to me. Their letters currently reside in my special file. I was grateful Trish took it upon herself to share the truth.

Teachable Moment: Commit to those who will not. Understand it requires a tremendous amount of granting grace and persevering with patience. If you find peers who truly have your best interests in mind, do not take those relationships for granted. Cherish them and understand the rarity in finding students or adults capable to stand up for what is right. In some instances, you will need all the strength of your soul to wait patiently for a positive outcome to a negative situation. It could take days or in the above case, two years, before you gain complete understanding of how the human dynamics played out. Be patient, committed and know if you maintained your integrity, good will prevail.

Character in Commitment: In Chapter 8, I shared the story about Frank becoming my knight in shining armor. I sensed the administration might punish him for being such a strong advocate for me. Frank was awarded the special opportunity to perform at graduation. Would the admin remove him due to his strong verbal objection to my forced retirement? When I visited with Frank about potentially losing this opportunity to sing, he replied immediately. He would sing plenty of times in the future. The administration could not silence him. I found it exhilarating to witness such fierce character in an 18 year old. Perhaps if students witness a teacher's dedication, this instills a like commitment to insure the teacher's honor.

Have No Fear in Pushing the Envelope: I began requiring retreats for my choirs in middle school. In order to foster an exemplary program, students on stage needed to connect with their fellow performers. This was accomplished through sharing their stories, openly demonstrating support of one another and a desire to perform at the highest level. Kids couldn't fake those attributes, so I wanted them to get to know each other on a deeper level. The once a year retreat required a three-hour stint, where the singers and I met at someone's home with the sole purpose to build relationships. The first hour involved eating and playing trust games. Then discussion of goals for each other and for the choir took place. The final hour we unmasked. Most of us wear a "mask" to school pretending everything is "just fine". The students agreed to share something about themselves, which no one probably knew. The one rule prevailed: you could not share a private family matter. In those discussions, students allowed their peers to experience their vulnerable side. Tears often presented themselves towards the end of the retreat regarding grand parents' deaths, parent divorces, problems with school or just teen issues in general. I never suggested my students hug each other. But it became a natural response. Students spent three hours with their choir mates, heard their pain, watched their tears and wanted to console one another. The process netted great results. Those kids genuinely cared for each other. If children loved one another unconditionally, they granted grace when their peers could not always meet expectations. It felt so gratifying to witness those 15 years of retreat experiences at the middle school. Those choirs performed on state, regional and national stages. Their public performances soared well beyond their years. I believe the correlation between great performances and knowing each other's journeys made a significant impact on their success. The authenticity of the performance became substantiated in their love for one another.

When I moved into the collegiate level, I tried the retreats there as well. I prepared myself for failure but to my amazement, the students received the retreat time as an opportunity to visit with peers outside the classroom. Friendships garnered for life. Face Book gave testimony to the lasting relationships forged in choir.

My college choir started out incredibly strong with great performers. Katie began running late or absent from rehearsals. This led to her absence from a performance, missing her assigned solo. When I inquired post concert why she neglected her responsibility to the choir, she became defensive and stormed off. A scheduled retreat ensued several days later. At the final hour, Katie shared she witnessed a drive by shooting and ultimate murder of her cousin. An awkward silence overcame everyone as she related the devastating story. Did this excuse Katie from neglecting future choir performances? No. But it helped all of us understand Katie's life experiences impacted her at such a level that commitment might not exist in her vocabulary. When she began to feel needed through the choir friendships, she became a better member. As her mentors, the students gently reminded her not to miss future rehearsals or concerts because they needed her. Retreats worked at all levels.

When I returned to teaching high school, I once again announced the required retreats. As a new concept, it caused some balking at the time commitment. I challenged the students. If I didn't literally push them out the door because they didn't want to leave when the retreat concluded, we would never hold another one. My bet would be won since the last hour's impact on everyone in attendance produced a lingering effect with no one wishing to leave.

The first retreat boasted great success, and at 5:30 pm I gently reminded them to go home. No one wanted to leave. Based on the outcome of yearly retreats, I began to theorize: bullied, angry or loner students could benefit from a retreat such as those. What if violence-prone children shared their fears and frustrations in a safe place, mentored by caring peers and adults? Every year, several of my disenfranchised students would tell me they planned on leaving our school until the retreat. I held the retreats within the first 45 days of the start of the school year to insure its positive effect.

Unfortunately, Jeanine did not believe the retreats as beneficial. She transferred in from another school her senior year and could not see herself as coerced to attend some random event. She complained, but I insisted she attend. Jeanine not only came to the retreat, she openly participated. She witnessed the positive outcome, which should have quelled her concern. But Jeanine's negative wiring got the best of her.

A few days after the retreat, the principal once again summoned me and asked why I held retreats. Thinking my principal would compliment me on the extra time spent with students, I gladly shared my philosophy. After all, I felt sure I would receive an accolade for going out of my way to reach out to my students. Instead, the principal scolded me with the condescending statement that I did not possess a guidance counselor certification. She concluded that students should not share their innermost thoughts in my presence. She also insinuated it could be perceived I dabbled in unsuitable relationships with my students. By the end of the conversation, I came to recognize Jeanine as the complainant, since the principal echoed her exact words. The principal banned the out of school retreats.

The students grew upset at the disallowing of the gatherings, and several parents offered to speak to the principal to seek change. I hadn't realized until those conversations the parents advocated for the retreats and wanted them to continue. They thought it most unfair the retreats canceled due to one complaint. Sending in parents to the principal about a problem usually made the situation worse, so I cautioned them not to contact the principal. With the retreats officially banned, the choir program's philosophy of creating a family like atmosphere fell victim to a knee jerk reaction principal. As the years transpired after the cancelation of retreats, I witnessed firsthand the void between my students. No commonality existed, as they never walked in each other's shoes and did not understand the closeness forged from trusting another human with their personal story. Ironically, I later discovered one of our school clubs held an annual off campus retreat, and so did several of the sports teams. But Jeanine would not be mollified, so the principal folded.

Teachable Moment: I hold no regrets for thinking outside of the box, granting grace to those students who chose not to board my creative ideas train, or constantly defending my teaching practices. But it took a tremendous sense of commitment and many days of prayer to sustain a long-term career.

When to Work the Rule: Commitment could take its toll. In the 80's I belonged to a teachers' association, which had the reputation of producing positive arbitration results. A salary impasse stymied the school board, central administration and the association. The teacher representatives decided all teachers should "work the rule." Teachers reported to their jobs 30 minutes before their classes began, taught throughout the day and left 30 minutes post the final class. No tests given, no homework assigned. Extracurricular activities, clubs, rehearsals, or practices postponed. The community needed to understand how much time their teachers worked outside the school day. After almost two weeks, the board felt pressured by the parents to end this stalemate and find a salary compromise, which they did.

Working the rule became a powerful tool when negotiating. The majority of the staff, in order for the shortened day to produce an impact on the administration and parents, must agree to participate. This approach challenged those of us who gladly gave extra time and energy to our jobs. Perhaps "work the rule" would better facilitate the impending teacher strikes. Keeping students in a routine, providing working parents a safe place for their children and understanding that strikes punish the student more than anyone would ease the tension caused by strikes.

Transfusion Time: If you give life blood to any job, you could end up bleeding to death. On those hectic concert/contest preparation weeks, I fantasized resting in a comfortable hospital bed. This pristine white building, in the middle of a quiet forest, provided me shelter from the weary world. Everyone would speak softly, and the ideal day included 12 hours of uncontested sleep. When my spirit deteriorated to that point, Time insisted I find ways to replace all the life blood I willingly donated. Otherwise, Music would never thrive in me and my sputtering flame could not cast any light outwards.

First and foremost, try not to take plan and grade books home. When our child left home to attend college, my husband knew supporting my passion to teach would produce the best outcome for our relationship. So the temptation to labor every night and on weekends created a catch-22 situation. I could not find the power to break the cycle of unending work. No one noticed the crazy hours I chalked up to providing a better experience for my students. When it came to teacher assessments, no one cared about the extra time I willingly gave to insure the student outcome showed growth exponentially. Why should any non-education professional, paid three times more, be able to come home at the end of the day and enjoy down time when a teacher cannot afford that luxury?

Use your vacation days for vacations. The summers exist for your family and not for a rigorous attempt to prepare your classroom. Your students will come and go. The family is on permanent assignment to remain with you a lifetime. This will not lessen your commitment but instead will strengthen it. Take a break!

Try to change the scenery. If opportunities present themselves to attend conferences, take them. Getting out of my routine and taking a breather helped alleviate some of the potential burn out stress. Join professional organizations and travel on behalf of your school. An extended weekend to converse with others in your field and lifting your head up from your plan book will help insure positive emotional and mental health.

Stressful times moved me to take advantage of procuring a mental health day to recover. I never required more than a couple per semester. Working feverishly up to that date, knowing there would be a break ahead, allowed me to pace myself. Commitment is an action verb for teachers who truly believe they can make a difference in a child's life. Ultimately it means: teaching for life and not stepping stones to a "better" position; having a tremendous amount of patience for those students who may not see eye to eye with your practices; seeking the most creative ideas to enhance learning and never allowing naysayers to detract you from your life's pursuit. *Teaching should be such that what is offered is perceived as a valuable gift and not as a hard duty.* — Albert Einstein

REFLECTION QUESTIONS

STUDENT

1. How do you perceive the difference between a dedicated teacher and one who merely fulfills the minimum requirements?
2. What attributes do teachers hold who show commitment to their profession?
3. Can someone be a committed teacher and still be disliked by their students? If yes, why?
4. Have you experienced teachers who maintained excellence in their commitment, but yet you could not connect with them? If yes, why?

PARENT

1. How do you perceive the difference between a dedicated teacher and one who merely fulfills the minimum requirements?
2. What attributes do teachers hold who show commitment to their profession?
3. Can someone be a committed teacher and still be disliked by your child? If yes, how?
4. Have you experienced teachers who maintained excellence in their commitment, but yet your child could not connect with them? If yes, why?

TEACHER

1. How do you perceive the difference between a dedicated colleague and one who merely fulfills the minimum requirements?
2. What attributes do colleagues hold who show commitment to their profession?
3. Can someone be a committed colleague and still be disliked by students? If yes, how?

4. Have you experienced colleagues who maintained excellence in their dedication, but students could not connect with them? If yes, why?
5. Where do you rate yourself? Committed? Doing only what is required? Sometimes both?

ADMINISTRATOR

1. How do you perceive the difference between a dedicated teacher and one who merely fulfills the minimum requirements?
2. What attributes do teachers hold who show commitment to their profession?
3. Can someone be a committed teacher and still be disliked by students? If yes, how?
4. Have you experienced teachers who maintained excellence in their commitment, but students could not connect with them? If yes, why?

CHAPTER 10: ROCKY ROAD IS NOT JUST A NAME FOR ICE CREAM!

Count it all joy, my brothers, when you meet trials of various kinds, for you know that the testing of your faith produces steadfastness. And let steadfastness have its full effect, that you may be perfect and complete, lacking in nothing. James 1:2-4

Those Boots Weren't Made for Teaching: Aaron, a first grader, toured the parameters of the room on a dead run as I prepared his class for their music time. With a twinkle in his eyes, he galloped around our circle of children and refused my request to join his classmates, seated on the floor. My sitting on a chair made for a first grader, wearing a skirt, presented its usual challenges. Today proved no exception. I coaxed Aaron to sit on the floor by me, which he reluctantly did. As I tried to capture the class' attention, Aaron became mesmerized with my patent leather, calf length boots. He touched them with one hand, squealed with delight and pulled his hand away. I asked him nicely to keep his hands to himself and join the rest of the children in singing. Unfortunately, his staccato touch gave way to running his hand up and down my boots. As I gallantly entwined my legs to steady myself on the small chair, I leaned over and firmly grabbed his hand and placed it by his side. The abatement of Aaron's hand on my boots failed once again. Of course, two hands could cover more territory on the shiny footwear, so his behavior spiraled out of control as both hands frantically moved over my boots.

My patience ended! With consternation, I looked into the deep, brown eyes of this seven-year old, and commanded him to take a chair. I grabbed the nearest chair and planted it directly behind him. Placing my unyielding hands on his shoulders, I slammed his derrière into the chair. Unfortunately, my aim of his derrière and the chair did not align. Aaron took a tumble straight to the ground. He wasn't physically hurt and thankfully he didn't cry. But the glance he shot me said it all. Why did this teacher, who seemed kind and loving, hurl him to the floor in disgust? How could that even happen?

On the way home that day, I prayed to God out loud in my car: Please forgive me for losing my temper with this little boy. I will never touch another child in anger again. The year was 1971. Forty-six years later, thankfully, I am able to state I kept true to my promise. Days existed when I felt my Solomon-like wisdom and patience drained from my very being. The lesson I learned from Aaron became my credo: I must never lose my patience with any child again. How did I refrain from emotional outbursts when a child's behavior became unreasonable? It's all about breathing!

In With The Good, Out With the Bad: When I learned Lamaze (natural child birth), the nurse stated anyone with an opera singing background already knew how to do Lamaze breathing. I trained as an opera singer, yet it became obvious these new breathing skills lacked from my coaching. The technique involved inhaling slowly through the nose as the stomach is pushed out (pressing against the belt buckle area). As the air is exhaled, the breath slowly traveled through my mouth in a hissing sound. The hissing sound could be replaced by quiet breathing through a pretend small straw. Exhaling should take at least 15 to 20 seconds. Determined to have natural child birth, I embraced this methodology early in my pregnancy. I controlled my breath, which ultimately slowed my heart rate. During the birth of our son, I proceeded through the entire event without drugs. I felt so empowered possessing this breathing technique. But I truly underestimated its importance in my life until controlling my emotional response under pressure became my focus.

My baby and I enjoyed our first two days together at home. But then something terrible and miraculous transpired. Probably due to stress and deprivation of sleep, I accidentally laid my open hand on a heated burner. The immediate pain seared through my entire palm. When I jerked my hand up, the red coils of the stove appeared as an outline on my palm. Through absolutely no thought process, my immediate reaction took me into Lamaze breathing. It didn't lessen the pain, but it helped me deal with it. Through the Lamaze method, my response to pain became a learned behavior.

In my early years of teaching, I easily found myself in tears if anyone confronted me. My emotions appeared uncontrollable. The more I tried to keep in check the tears and vocal tremor, the worse it became. I couldn't utter more than a brief response due to hyperventilated breathing and palpitating heart rate. When a parent or administrator demanded answers and my only response came out with a sniveling voice and teary eye, my effectiveness as a teacher materialized into a diminished, unconfident shell of a person. Whether it became a purposeful response or quite by accident, I began using this breathing technique with all confrontations or pressure-filled moments.

Occasionally feelings could get hurt and in rare cases, trampled by a student who forgot to speak with a filter. The sporadic hostility forged in the classroom mortified me as a young teacher. Over the years, I found inhaling slowly (in with the good) and exhaling slowly (out with the bad) became a positive first response to such situations. On that final EOY day, with rants which reduced my very spirit, I never cried or felt emotional overload. Without even thinking, I found myself breathing deeply and evenly. I felt in control of my breathing, heart rate, voice and emotions. It did not make the pain of hurtful words diminish, but it helped the even handed response I provided.

Teachable Moment: Controlled breathing from the lower intercostal muscles, one of the tenants of yoga, insures a true cleansing breath. Spending at least five to ten minutes per day on this technique reinforced my ability to become more reliant on this procedure. I used it in auditions, job interviews, physical illness and emotional trauma. I teach it today to my voice students. This controlled response is not just a singer's breathing technique, but also a coping mechanism.

Profanity Reflects A Loss of Control: Sheryl personified cool. In her 50's, charismatic and wonderfully skilled in teaching History, Sheryl also possessed a sailor's mouth. I heard her across the hallway, dropping the F bomb, as she casually visited with her students. I startled at the word and looked to see if any of her students exhibited signs of upset from the language use. On the contrary, students perceived Sheryl as a hip teacher, who could relate to them on their level. She received reverence in her classroom and held in high esteem by the administration. Why did parents lodge frivolous complaints against some teachers, and yet appeared silent when it came to teachers' use of profanity in the classroom? The demise of civil language and acceptance of profanity laced speech outside of the classroom has, unfortunately, cultivated degrading and unintelligent language into the classroom. Using an easy four-letter curse word took no thought. Using a euphemism of the thoughts which needed to be conveyed in place of the profanity demonstrated much more intelligence and self control.

My classroom language morphed over the years. When I first started teaching, I never thought to speak a "hell" or a "damn" in the classroom. But when I needed to confront Charlene about her rudeness, my breathing never kicked in nor did my composure.

Charlene, the editor of the school newspaper, learned about the complexities of freedom of the press first hand. She possessed exemplary writing skills which manifested themselves in her position as the esteemed student editor. One of her first stories of the year was based on interviews with students who auditioned and did not gain acceptance into higher choirs. This proved a challenge for my initiation into the academic year. Never afforded advance notice to the questions asked, I definitely did not grant her permission to hold those interviews. My sole job became picking up the pieces of our choir program after the paper published the audition accounts. No one escaped unscathed in that journalism piece. The students who auditioned successfully came across as villains. The students who were not selected for an advanced choir became victims, wallowing in their self-pity. Our choir rehearsals became nonexistent due to the blowback from the story. The students needed to use class time to vent about the disparaging article. I approached the staff sponsor and asked if she could arbitrate the chaos created from the story. The sponsor forwarded my concerns to Charlene, but that would be the extent of her intervention.

Miss Charlene came sashaying into my office two hours later. She appeared as someone about to confidently argue the freedom of the press with aplomb. I asked if she realized her story hurt many feelings, which in turn created three days of nonexistent rehearsals. Charlene smiled, cocked her head and retorted the story needed to be told. After all, freedom of the press appeared in her corner. My Darth Vader voice spewed forth with no filter. I reminded Miss Charlene she was the editor of a high school newspaper and not the *New York Times*.

She and her freedom of the press could go straight to hell! Those words even surprised me as they poured out with no premeditated thought. Luckily the unreported episode never gained administration attention.

Teachable Moment: Students know how and when to push teachers' emotional buttons. It is paramount we teachers do not respond in kind. I held my composure over these past decades until this last year, when a student accused me and my students of being devil worshippers due to lyrics in our songs. The anger I displayed in that situation revealed as measured and controlled, with no profanity in my response. This same student adhered to the theory the earth is flat and aborted fetus tissue is placed in soft drinks. His accusations now seem almost humorous except for the fact the administration gave these allegations legitimacy by calling me in to explain the meanings of the songs selected. I found, via the internet, literary professors explaining the lyrics to our repertoire as quite innocent. The administration could have proceeded to do the same search, but calling me in appeared a better way to once again diminish my integrity.

Freedom From Information: In the 90's, I experienced a sudden health issue. After a day of teaching, I found myself in a curled up position on my bed, the pain searing through my very being. How could I come down sick with an impending major concert the following evening? A positive mindset stopped the pain periodically, but recovery would be impossible. At the emergency room, diagnosed with an inflamed gall bladder, I succumbed to the reality of immediate surgery. Not only would I be unable to conduct the special honorary concert, I would be absent from school for a few days. Then the awful mind-numbing thought swept over me, which had nothing to do with the pain of a gall bladder. No plans existed for a last minute substitute!

The week previously, I purchased a new video featuring Bette Midler in *For the Boys*. An inspiring movie based on an aging fictional singer, the film depicted the singer contemplating her life-long career on the stage. It showcased music from Vaudeville through the 70's. Not only did it prove historical in its drama, but also demonstrated an educational reference for the music of each decade. Formulating plans for a sub to show the movie during my absence appeared the best solution. I recovered quickly and returned to the classroom in three days, just in time for the last 15 minutes of the movie.

I did not want to show the ending due to nonexistent rehearsal time. The students became verbal about their disappointment, so I decided it would be easier to show the 15 minute ending than moderate a 20 minute argument. Seeing the students genuinely loved the film also reinforced presenting the movie proved a sound educational idea.

The movie began and within minutes, the word "shit" permeated the air. Shock went through me! How could this be a PG-13 movie? I moved swiftly to switch the movie off, but the kids pleaded with me to see the ending. I acquiesced only to hear the F word a short time later. I marched to the VCR and turned it off. There in front of me lay the VCR cover for the movie, with the R rating plainly in sight. Due to the emergency of my surgery, I had not taken the time to insure the movie PG-13. My apology for showing the film came forthwith. The students assured me they heard much worse. I reminded them that in the public school classroom, profane language was inappropriate and unacceptable. We moved on and put the awkward situation behind us. Or so I thought.

Teachers love their unregimented summertime and most always administrators understand their role not to intrude. So when my principal phoned me at home in July, I knew immediately this intrusion was mandated by a serious matter.

Sam asked me very calmly if I ever showed an R rated movie to my classes. My past caught up with me! I explained I thought the movie to be PG13 and requested it shown when I went into emergency surgery. I further related I apologized to the students and refused to let them see the ending of the film when I found out it contained an R rating. Then Sam shared with me what transpired.

My sub wrote a letter to the editor of our city's newspaper and stated she was forced to show an R rated movie in my classroom. This sub felt appalled I would allow my students to see such a movie. How did my principal react? No standard response of admonishment came forth. Instead, Sam demonstrated the attributes of a great administrator. He listened to my explanation, understood the context of the situation and granted me grace. He trusted me. Sam allowed me to make a mistake because he knew my intentions were never to overtly break rules. My 13 year tenure with Sam proved the best in my career as an educator. When most future administrators would find it challenging to support me, I gratefully reflected on my time with Sam. As far as my sub writing the letter, my principal called the superintendent and explained the situation, defending me in the process. The superintendent withdrew the sub's right to teach in our district, thus omitting her permanently from the substitute pool. Justice served, but not at my expense.

Teachable Moment: Make sure you are using educational supplements which are appropriate for your students. Most districts provide set guidelines. When in doubt, ask. If you make a mistake, own up to it and do what it takes to move on. The sub should have turned off the movie for its language and called me immediately for alternate plans.

Knee Jerk Reactions: A few years ago, as we prepared for our concert, a singer came to me claiming she spotted one of our performers drinking alcohol in a practice room. This accusation presented itself seven minutes before our start time. I immediately went to the practice room, found the small liquor bottle in the wastebasket and began to hunt down the vice-principal, who attended the evening's concert. He immediately found the culprit, assured me everything was fine, and the concert began only a few minutes late.

A small group performed on stage while I took my position back stage. In the darkness of stage left, I literally stumbled into our principal, Jan. She possessed a facial expression which caused me to stop dead in my tracks. It became apparent Jan did not make the effort to meet me backstage to compliment me for the fine concert at hand. Instead she informed me more students participated in pre-concert alcohol than originally thought. I felt stunned, as I thought the situation over and handled by the vice-principal. Jan asked me to round up one of our boys, Tim, because his name was given as drinking with the other boy. Instead of directing my concert, I found myself tip-toeing through the kids standing back stage in search of Tim. I found him a few minutes later and sent him to the waiting principal so I could enter the stage to direct the choir. Instead of concentrating on the music, my confusion and ultimate anger resonated because of the surprise appearance of the principal backstage. Not only did she never support me in anything, but in most cases her behavior towards me appeared openly hostile. I felt sure this would turn ugly. And it did.

By mid-concert, the principal cornered me and asked me to find two additional students. Rumors started circulating that the entire choir department (150+) was drunk. The student leadership immediately moved into support mode. They felt equally angry about the prospect of kids using alcohol before a concert and asked fellow students to breathe on them to see if alcohol could be detected. I could see this event ending my career.

I stopped caring about the concert. At one point, I stepped in front of the choir on stage, smiled and asked them what song they were performing. My brain throbbed on overload, trying to make sense out of this impending disaster. Peripherally, I could see Jan hovering over my students in the darkened backstage. When she finally stepped into the light of the hallway, I witnessed her frazzled brunette hair flying in every direction. She came dressed with no makeup, donning an old t-shirt with faded jeans and flip flops. Jan looked as if she literally jumped out of bed to direct this debacle. She informed me she would make a public announcement before the end of the program: all singers must meet with her post concert. I agreed to her request, still numb how this could have escalated into a career ending crisis.

The concert over, Jan took to the stage appearing most unprofessional. This disheveled creature stammered about how no singer would be allowed to join their parents until after a required meeting. Dismissing the students to the appointed meeting place, the auditorium emptied in complete awkward silence. She then informed me that police were stationed at every door and would be giving breathalyzer tests to all students. You cannot make this up. While the incident needed to be taken seriously, bringing two administrators on site, calling the police, locking the outside doors and threatening breathalyzer tests definitely constituted a knee jerk reaction.

When I gathered all the singers together, Jan did not appear. We waited 10 minutes for her arrival. She explicitly told me I could not share with the singers why they could not leave the room. Kids appeared visibly upset and demanded why they needed to sit on a cold floor, in an empty room, waiting for a principal for no apparent reason. Jan finally made her entrance. She ended up waiting in the wrong room. It begs the question: how do people like this receive administrative positions? When she informed the students about the situation, mindful I thought the singers would all undergo breathalyzer tests, she simply stated some poor decisions were made and we could now all go home. In the aftermath, I learned three of my instrumentalists made the decision to drink alcohol before the concert. Instead of fact finding, the knee jerk reaction led to the assumption that all the kids must be drunk.

Teachable Moment: I did learn a very good lesson from this. It was not humanly possible to run a concert with 150+ students with no adult help. From that evening on, my parent volunteers staffed our concerts from the tech rehearsal to the final moment of tearing down the stage. Wonderfully assertive, the parents helped immensely. They initiated conversations with students who appeared headed in the wrong direction. I could relax before the concert, at least to some degree, knowing these parents would be patrolling the halls, bathrooms and practice rooms.

Emails Are Not for the Faint-of-Heart: Parents questioning a teacher at parent/teacher conferences is certainly acceptable. In the 21st century however, emailing parents push "send" knowing said angry email could result in a teacher feeling attacked and disrespected. This way of communicating is permitted, if only due to the administration's reputation of seldom defending the targeted teacher. Carbon copying the administration became another way of ensuring a teacher experienced the full import of parental wrath. Fact finding seldom considered. The assumption? Teenagers come readily equipped to report accurately anything which transpires. These children not only received the green light to air their opinions about how a classroom, audition, rehearsal, practice or game should be managed, but their viewpoints ended up receiving validation by spineless administrators. If the child stated it and the parent emailed it, then the teacher must be guilty.

I learned some good techniques in dealing with this type of attack:

1. Do not respond to an angry email until you take at least a few hours to recover from the attack.
2. Do not lay out the entire scenario of what happened. Instead write an even handed, short response. If the parent carbon copied the admin, make sure they receive the response as well.
3. State the facts. Answer any accusations with an unbiased account.
4. If the email is filled with misrepresentations, reply you could not possibly respond to all of the claims and request the parent to set up a meeting with you and your admin representative as soon as possible. Many times parents will not follow through, as this would force them to a face to face meeting.
5. Never agree to a one on one meeting with an upset parent. Ask a facilitator to take notes on any meeting which holds the potential for turning negative.
6. Respond to all emails within 24 hours.
7. Never take out your frustration on the child of the irate parent. In some cases, the parent never told the child about the angry email or the child held no control over the parent. Go out of your way to treat the student of the offending parent with the highest regard possible. It proves challenging yet

empowering to know you can refrain from stooping to the infuriated parent's level.

8. Returning a venomous response to an already inflammatory situation will worsen and elongate the resolve.

9. Be proactive. Keeping a website with all of the information is paramount to warding off parents who have nothing better than to question you at every turn. Publish a handbook with all perceived problems included.

10. Share with the administration all documents regarding rules, regulations, expectations and syllabi.

Do not take the attack personally (much easier given in advice than received in practice). This proves itself the most challenging response. When a parent said I was the reason their child would never sing again or I failed at encouraging their child, I needed to remember abrasive parents are also products of their own environment. Unhappy parents, with impending life changes, misdirect their anger and frustration. They find a soft target, shoot arrows of hurt and placate themselves with the entitlement philosophy.

Teachable Moment: I experienced many parents attacked teachers when they felt helpless in their own life situation. Divorced, spouse militarily deployed, or unemployed parents could become systemically negative. Parents do not wish to deal with the perceived notion their child is not happy in the classroom. It must be the fault of the teacher. When dealing with irrational accusations, I became mindful I was not the target. I happened to be standing in front of it.

Social Media Madness: It is troubling, when today's founders of some of the most used social media sites actually end up resigning from the use of their own platforms. The internet teems with unspeakable events and pictures. The reliability of truth on the worldwide web diminishes every time a site manipulates and forges unhealthy ideas for our children. Facts often get skewed. Reported "news" looks like the tabloids of yesteryear. We face ever increasing challenges wading through the mire of social media facts and fiction.

Students gaining permission to use sites where they can post an insensitive picture or say disparaging comments, knowing the post will stay up only a matter of minutes truly boggles the mind. Parents need to monitor these sites on a daily basis to insure their children do not face bullying or initiate the bullying themselves. Unfortunately, when a student uses social media to bully someone, the act itself appears as heroic by his peers. How "cool" to level a salvo at another human being and get the act erased by a program specializing in making a minimal footprint! But the hurt stays, unable to abate.

What best conveys social media? The mighty mobile device proves itself a major player in the social media game. Phones, growing out of students' hands, can lead to much destruction. Some of the drama created in my classes revolved around a lost or stolen phone. Then in their divine wisdom, districts started a BYOD (Bring Your Own Device) program. Student requirements included bringing their laptops, iPads or mobile phones to every class. They would joke amongst themselves how easy texting their friends became during class. With their mobile device in plain sight, the temptation to use it for other means remained with them every hour of every day. The forced reliance of today's teachers on websites in their class presentations truly creates a sad picture. My administrator constantly harangued me for avoiding 21st century technology because I did not wish to use apps in my teaching.

According to Tom Kersting, the author of *Disconnected*, the increase of kids having anxiety, ADD, ADHD demonstrates how the internet is affecting human behavior. Seth Wenig, a

Reuters contributor, reported it should not come as a surprise that Silicon Valley parents are strict about technology use with their children. Yet public schools, by their decrees of reliance on the world web, inundate our children with electronic screens.

Teachable Moment: Parents and teachers need to maintain vigilance. My students shared how they used their phones at 3 a.m. playing games, exchanging texts and surfing the web. Our educational system should push pause and evaluate if technology really proves the best choice when delivering today's preeminent teaching practices. Why would it be more beneficial for a student to receive his academic tutorials from the entertaining internet sites instead of an actual live presentation? Could the constant presence of the internet find correlation with increased school violence?

Walk Up, Not Out: Watching the aftermath of the Parkland shootings with 14 children and three teachers shot in cold blood, I continually searched my soul for an answer. To be sure, one answer does not suffice. However, when it comes to the safety of our children, the answer must dictate a non-partisan approach. Our country bears an obligation to shelter our children and teachers from the violence which permeates our culture and our schools, much of it generated through social media.

Alaina Petty, 14 years old, was one of the victims of the Parkland shootings. Her father, Ryan Petty, started a new movement which spun out of the "Walk Out" rallies. His movement entitled *Walk up, Not Out* persuades all of us to action instead of just tweeting other's ideas or holding signs at a rally. *Walk Up, Not Out* addresses one of the largest in scope issues facing our school systems today. Kids feel isolated, under attack and unable to deal with the madness of social media. Mr. Petty posted on Twitter: "Instead of walking out of school, encourage students to walk up. Walk up to the kid who sits alone at lunch and invite him to sit with your group; walk up to the kid who sits quietly in the corner of the room and sit next to her. Walk up to your teachers and thank them; walk up to someone who has different views than you and get to know them -- you may be surprised at how much you have in common."

For years I sponsored a club *Friends of Rachel*, which was similar to Ryan Petty's proposal. Rachel Scott was the first student killed during the Columbine High School rampage of 1999. She left an incredible legacy of simple acts of kindness. Rachel's Challenge (*Friends of Rachel clubs*) was described by Dr. Robert Marzano as "one of the most powerful interventions I have seen in 40 years of working in education." I served as a witness to that very statement.

When the *Rachel's Challenge* presentation came to our school, I felt deeply impacted, more so than with any other assembly I attended in the past. A slide presentation presented by her brother demonstrated how Rachel genuinely cared for her fellow students. She cared, not in words, but by actions. When the hour presentation finished, many of us wept. Evil tried to kill the goodness in this young woman, but it could not. In her death, many students felt moved to make a change. To date, her story reached 25 million people across the globe. It provides a foundation for creating programs which promote a positive climate in K-12 schools. People who strive to light the world in the midst of darkness kindle my flame even more.

Two years later Rachel's Challenge made a repeat presentation. We took the tenants of *Friends of Rachel* and ran with it again. As with most crisis events, time not only heals, but it also can erase memories. We tried to keep the club moving forward but in three years, most of our students had not experienced the original slide show and speaker. The administration chose not to spend the several thousand dollars for a third appearance. Membership dwindled each year. Our club lasted almost six years, which seemed more effective than most high schools. Then the administration hammered in the final nail to the club's demise.

High school clubs constantly receive warnings by central administrations to orient their goals towards curriculum-based concepts. I believe this overzealous approach began when Christian students' clubs sued and in some places won their right to access high school campuses. In my opinion, to avoid further controversy, public schools found a way to skirt this issue by insisting all clubs be curriculum-based, thereby creating an impossible circumstance for Christian clubs to exist. A classic knee-jerk reaction.

The assistant principal met with me before school started in the fall to relay *Friends of Rachel* would no longer receive recognition as a school sponsored club. How did this translate? No public announcement (either on the intercom or on posters) allowed. Funding removed, and the $300 in our account subsequently frozen proved an insurmountable challenge. Our students tried diligently to get the word out about our meetings, but to little success. Over five years, our numbers depleted from 90 students to a handful. Student leadership became disheartened, since it appeared our administration went out of its way to discourage membership to *Friends of Rachel*. I asked the staff if anyone might be willing to breathe new life into the club because fresh ideas did not exist. No one stepped forward. No school shootings occurred in recent times, so complacency abounded.

An administrative suggestion came forth that *Friends of Rachel* could solve the curriculum-based problem if the chapter would undergo reorganization and utilize the health class curriculum. I received a one-inch thick health book in August and told as soon as I could readjust our club to conform, we could receive school sponsorship. Our choir program continued to increase during those five years so finding time to redesign and rewrite a charter, just as school started, overwhelmed me. The club was not destined to survive. By December of that year, we finally stopped meeting due to lack of interest and no way to communicate.

The following May, one of the administrators came to me with an apology. *Friends of Rachel* indeed received support from the district, therefore it did not need to meet the curriculum-based requirement. How did I react to that information? With contempt for an administration who acted without fact finding and not advocating for the students. The administrative premature destruction of the club resulted in no students or faculty stepping forward to take the reins.

Complacency becomes an issue with any program which attempts to change the thinking and actions of our children. Programs like *Walk Up, Not Out* and *Friends of Rachel* should not be allowed to end due to restrictions or lack of financial support by administrations. Our memories possess an incredible ability to shelve violent acts to the far recesses of our minds. The horrors of 911 diminished through time. I visited the memorial in New York City three times and found something new which moved me more than the previous visit. What if positive action programs existed which received reinforcement every year? What if the monthly curriculum included time for students to feel connected?

Remember the choir retreats, canceled by the limited vision principal? Those three hours changed kids' lives. It changed my life every time. Our educational priorities need to refocus. This is no longer the society or school system of our grandfathers. Family centered support structure for many of our children does not exist. Does the role of schools include acting as the replacement for missing in action parents? No. But schools could create a safer environment if time were spent growing the child emotionally as well as academically. Teaching and demonstrating traits of The Golden Rule would foster students' emotional and academic growth exponentially. Implementing those retreats, while challenging to schedule, would demonstrate an outcome to warrant their existence. I am proposing a onetime gathering, made up of small groups of students, at the beginning of the academic year. Staff would take three hours to encourage their students to know one another on a more personal level. What if we used "professional development" days to insure the sanctity of our students' school experiences rather than sitting in meetings scheduled to justify an administrator's salary? If one to two days per year would help the isolated, hate filled kids to find a connection, wouldn't the time spent outweigh the challenge of logistics? If a few hours could stop one more child from dying in a school shooting, why wouldn't all educators support it? It might not prove itself the end-all, but it could serve as a springboard for schools encouraging children to thrive instead of staying home because they see their school as a hostile environment.

We cannot accept the slaughter of innocent children as byproduct of the culture! A nationally mandated law should be implemented requiring a yearly program which affords children a proven plan of action where they will feel safe, connected and supported. To affect change immediately, Teacher's Colleges need to implement teaching practices which include a new approach to interacting with students. All teachers should equip themselves with positive teaching methods when dealing with those children who flounder in the daily shuffle. Administrators should encourage their staff to reach out to lost kids. Never should principals admonish teachers for going out of their way to insure a child's stable emotional health. If the retreats could take the place of the mind numbing, ineffectual professional development meetings, I believe there would be much more buy-in power. Student assessments will not show growth if our children and teachers fear for their lives when they enter their classrooms. Overhearing my students sharing with new singers that our choir program felt like being a member of a family proved some of the best moments I experienced as a teacher. In most cases, the angry school shooter was void of familial support nor was he in possession of a moral compass. He barely functioned in the school environment designed for emotionally stable children.

One of the most positive posts on Face Book, regarding the Parkland massacre, came from Kelly Guthrie Raley, named the teacher of the year in the same district where the Parkland killings took place. A portion of what she said: "Okay, I'll be the bad guy and say what no one else is brave enough to say, but wants to say. I'll take all the criticism and attacks from everyone because you know what? I'm a TEACHER. I live this life daily. And I wouldn't do anything else! But I also know daily I could end up in an active shooter situation." "Until we, as a country, are willing to get serious and talk about mental health issues, lack of available care for the mental health issues, lack of discipline in the home, horrendous lack of parental support when the schools are trying to control horrible behavior at school (oh no! Not MY KID. What did YOU do to cause my kid to react that way?), lack of moral values, and yes, I'll say it -- violent video games that take away all sensitivity to ANY compassion for others' lives, as well as reality TV that makes it commonplace for people to constantly scream up in each others' faces and not value any other person but themselves, we will have a gun problem in school. Our kids don't understand the permanency of death anymore!!!"

Teachable Moment: Schools should demonstrate a proactive stance when insuring their children maintain a healthy connection with their teachers, as well as their peers. This new approach may need direction from state or national legislation to prohibit clubs like *Friends of Rachel* from dying out due to lack of support. Teachers already feel inundated with curriculum requirements and some lack the empathy needed to deal with children's emotions. Administration hands will be tied to support such a movement, due to financial restraints. Therefore actions to improve the emotional environment need mandating and funding by legislation. A quote by Frederick Douglass holds truth: "It is easier to build strong children than to repair broken adults."

Secularism: Is It Working? Whose morals and whose God shall the public schools embrace? This statement continues to be the one which prohibits any conversation of bringing morals, decency and respect back into the classroom. In 1962, the Supreme Court asked the God of Christians and Jews to vacate the public schools. According to an article published in the *Examiner*, no one should be surprised by the results:

- Criminal arrest of teens is up 150% according to the US Bureau of Census.
- Teen suicides in ages 15-19 years up 450% according to the National Center of Health Services.
- Illegal drug activity is up 6000% according to the National Institute of Drug Abuse.
- Child abuse cases up 2300% according to the US Department of Health and Human Services.

- Divorce up 350% according to the US Department of Commerce.
- SAT scores fell 10% even though the SAT questions have been revamped to be easier to answer.
- Violent crime has risen 350%.
- National morality figures have plummeted, and teen pregnancy escalated dramatically.

Floundering in the sea of godlessness, our schools and culture lost its moral compass. If we believe these facts, they indicate the damning results of a society devoid of God. If you remain skeptical that the banning of God in our schools brought about the above statistics, I will attest the classrooms I taught in the 1970's through the 80's proved themselves kinder and gentler, and held far less drama than the classrooms of today. In my opinion, it will only worsen in a complacent society who continues to support curriculum with no moral direction.

Several weeks ago, my husband, who played and coached basketball, received recognition at his parochial high school in Indiana. We attended the festivities which concluded with a basketball game. My husband's alma mater played their arch rivals from across town. We rose for the National Anthem, followed by a prayer. Since the home team was a Lutheran high school, starting the game with prayer was permitted. I have attended hundreds of basketball games in support of my husband, son and grandchild. The environment of this one game felt unlike any of the others.

The public announcer presented the prayer articulately and with passion. The plea petitioned God to watch over this game, keeping players safe and assuring the play held no malice. The intensity displayed on the court made this game different. With fast, physical play, young men careened, sprawled on the floor. Yet no animosity between players or fans appeared at any time. Coaches did not rant or cuss at the referees. Young men played hard, but most importantly played fair. The opposing school brought with them a large contingency of fans, most of them African-American. Yet rival fans shouted no racial slurs and no black vs. white confrontations ensued. A sense of calm prevailed. Even though vigorous emotions displayed themselves on the court, I felt comfortable watching two teams battle for the win. Through prayer, the school invited God's presence at the start of the game. His attendance prevailed throughout the evening. I believe it made a difference.

Can we revisit the banning of God, Bible and prayer? We charted this course for over a half century. The results, arguably, made schools less safe. I am afraid our legislators remain too swayed by secular progressives, and our courts too biased to consider God a viable part of our culture. Could the following present a compromise? Could these proposals at least warrant a national discussion?

1. Parents who desire to send their children to parochial schools should be given tax credit and/or deductions if they cannot afford tuition.
2. Christian clubs should be allowed the same status as other clubs.
3. Christianity or any other religious beliefs should never be disparaged in the classroom in the name of curriculum study.
4. Student, teacher or coach led prayers, at any event, should be allowed as long as students voluntarily participate.
5. Biblical study should be allowed in any literature or historical study.

Christianity is not a threat to our schools. An exchange of opposing ideas should be celebrated instead of condemned.

Students and their teachers could agree to disagree and at the end of the day, find less hate and more commonality in their relationships.

When homeschooling began as a popular way of delivering education, I scoffed at it. A common belief persisted homeschooled students would be socially deprived and isolated from the real world. I changed my mind and understood completely those parents who wish to home school their children. These parents see our public schools as at least amoral and at the worst, immoral. Public school parents need to remain vigilant and advocate for their child's right to an unbiased education. Not the kind of parent who hides behind a computer to attack, but instead the omniscient parent who insures his child experiences a balanced curriculum, evenhanded discipline and a school wide program, which reinforces the Golden Rule.

Teachable Moment: Treating others as we wish to be treated, as simplistic as it sounds, could solve so many of the issues facing public education in a secular progressive society. You would not need to invoke God or any particular religion as the Golden Rule exists in all belief systems.

Traveling the rocky road of public education is not for the weak in stamina. I believe understanding the topography beforehand is paramount to the successful journey. There will be children who challenge your very existence. The days are plentiful when you reach the outer limits of your patience. Those around you will not always affirm you. The culture we live in is not conducive to human differences. Violence and hatred weave their grotesque threads throughout the human frailty. And there will be more school shootings. But you may be the one person, who possesses the potential to change all of that by reaching one lost child. *The mediocre teacher tells. The good teacher explains. The great teacher demonstrates. The superior teacher inspires.* —Willian A. Ward.

REFLECTION QUESTIONS:

STUDENT

1. Did your actions cause a teacher to be reprimanded? put on leave? fired?
2. Do students have the right to protest during school? Do teachers have the right to strike and/or protest? What are the consequences of each?
3. Do you use appropriate language in the classroom? Do your teachers?
4. Did you ever push a teacher to the brink of emotional distress? If yes, why?

PARENT

1. Did your actions cause a teacher to be reprimanded? put on leave? fired?
2. Do students have the right to protest during school? Do teachers have the right to strike and/or protest? What are the consequences of each?
3. Do you use appropriate language in your home? If yes, what consequences do you put in place if your children use inappropriate language?
4. Did you ever push a teacher to the brink of emotional distress? If yes, why?

TEACHER

1. Did you need to take a leave from your classroom due to parent or admin actions? Quit teaching? Hire an attorney? File a suit?
2. Do students have the right to protest during school? Do teachers have the right to strike and/or protest? What are the consequences of each?
3. Do you use appropriate language in your home? in the classroom?
4. Did you ever push a colleague to the brink of emotional distress? If yes, why?

ADMINISTRATOR

1. Did your actions cause a teacher to quit teaching?
2. Do students have the right to protest during school? Do teachers have the right to strike and/or protest? What are the consequences of each?
3. Do you use appropriate language in your home? at school?
4. Did you ever push a teacher to the brink of emotional distress? If yes, why?

CHAPTER 11: BEGGING THE QUESTIONS

Six months ago, I embarked on a writing journey unlike anything I ever attempted. Over decades of teaching, friends, family and colleagues encouraged me to write a book about my experiences in the classroom. The genesis, a memoir in the making, morphed into something much greater: encouraging four different points of view to provide a kinder and gentler environment for teachers. As this revision slowly evolved, I encountered detours. Why should I share my experiences without adding solutions? How do I present a balanced exposé of both the challenging and the euphoric moments? Is it a memoire or a self-help treatise? How would my Christian beliefs affect a secular progressive audience?

I never foresaw my memoir including God's influence on my life until His still, soft voice entered into my writing. By Chapter 3, I began to perceive God walked with me throughout every day of my teaching career. But most assuredly my abiding faith since childhood guaranteed I knew of God's esteemed presence throughout my life as a teacher. But did I? Too many times I cried out to God how lost I felt, how compromised my integrity appeared at every juncture, and how He allowed bad things to happen to me. Was I being punished for my sins? This divine truth persists: God loved me and continues to love me unconditionally through every moment of challenge and hardship. Bad things entwined themselves throughout my journey, not by accident but by design. Not to punish me, but to hone and transform me into a better educator and eventually a resolute author. I give God the glory and to my incredible students, the credit for mentoring and uplifting me.

Every year my students selected themes to motivate our choir program. My most favorite one reflected my life as a teacher: From Charcoal to Diamond. The effervescent sparkle, created in my being, endured time, heat, and pressure. I falsely believed this metamorphic process ended upon my retirement. To my amusement and awe, discovering the aptitude for sharing my experiences on paper provides me with not only solace, but a resolve to participate in a discussion for marked change. Music transformed my soul and continually reignited the flame to grow young children into creative and productive adults. The story teller flicker, a small spark whetted from time, heat and pressure, invigorates my heart to embrace this new advocacy role.

One person holds the power to make a difference. With that hope in mind, I encourage the four points of view (students, parents, teachers and administrators) to advance the national dialogue regarding the respect owed our teachers. How do we accommodate that charge?

1. Teacher pedagogy classes at universities: After reading *Rescue the Teacher, Save the Child!* complete the questions at the conclusion of each chapter through small group conversations. Avoid the simple answer of "yes" or "no." Take time to role play in the different and sometimes opposing points of view. Empower yourselves now with vigilance for those who would attempt to undermine the role of teachers. Develop your cognitive skills and anticipate possible problems in your future teacher positions.

2. Teachers in the field (Middle School/High School/College): Use this book to initiate conversations with your students

regarding best teacher practices and eliciting empathy for one another's roles. The schools of the 21st century must catch up with the directional change mandated by social media. The printed syllabi cannot close the 21st century gap between teacher and student. Before one concept is taught, you and your students need to better understand your roles with transparent dialogue.

3. Parents: Implement this book at PTO/PTA meetings regarding how you could best support the teaching staff. Encouraging and even demanding positive parental communication produces the necessary precedence and pressure to behave judiciously.

4. Teacher Professional Development days: Complete the questions asked in previous chapters and this chapter. These sometimes dreaded days could transform relationships and afford a more inviting environment through open discussions. Equip one another, with a face to face scenario, to combat gossip mongering, false narratives and negative perceptions. Emails squelch open dialogue so desperately needed amongst staff. Ineffectual professional development days, designed by administrators to justify the school calendar and perhaps their own dissertation, leave staff depleted and discouraged.

5. *Rescue the Teacher, Save the Child!* could serve as a reference for anyone pursuing a career in disseminating knowledge, be it work place, school or church, Christian or secular. My post-teaching purpose includes writing, and more importantly speaking to those audiences who seek the best for our educators. Please visit my blog rescuetheteacher.com and share your ideas, thoughts and concerns.

As promised in Chapter 1, solutions exist in revitalizing the teaching profession. Please take time to answer the following questions and share points of view. In order to facilitate real and abiding change, these questions must be sincerely contemplated, openly discussed and answered. There are no "correct" responses. More than likely, most respondents have walked in at least two points of view. All points of view need to declare an abolition to the systemic defeatist attitudes expressed by those who do not value our teachers.

Student Questions:

1. In general, what feelings do I hold regarding my teachers? Respectful? Negative? Non-committal?
2. Do I work diligently in all of my classes? If not, why not?
3. Am I patient with my teachers when they speak?
4. How could I help my teachers feel successful?
5. When I am out of class, do I gossip about teachers, and encourage others to participate in said negative discussions?
6. Have I encouraged other students to act on their discontentment with their teachers? Sending accusatory emails? Writing anonymous notes?
7. When faced with a teacher whose philosophy or teaching practices I disagree with, how do I navigate the situation? Ignore it? Speak with the teacher directly?
8. Have I embellished the perceived negativity about my teachers to my parents? Give an example.
9. Do I encourage my parents to write angry emails? Confront the teacher in person? Go over the teacher's head to the administration?
10. Have I forged half truths about a teacher just because I didn't like that person? Give an example.
11. When a teacher is under attack, am I silent or do I try to defend the teacher?
12. Do I believe I deserve special treatment by my teachers?
13. Have I completed a random act of kindness for any of my teachers? Give an example.
14. Do I take the time to greet every teacher upon entering their classroom?

15. Have I dropped by a teacher's office at the end of the day just to chat?
16. When a teacher appears unfair, do I question it during the class or do I wait to question it privately?
17. Have I considered becoming a teacher? If yes, would this be a lifetime career? If no, why not?
18. When I do feel the need to correct a teacher, do I address the teacher in a respectful way?
19. Is there a way I am able to contribute to the national conversation to affirm teachers? If so, what might that look like?
20. Do I treat teachers the way I would like to be treated?

Parent Questions:
1. Do I openly speak negatively about my child's teacher in front of my child?
2. Have I publicly supported my child's teacher, even though I may not agree with some of the decisions made in his classroom?
3. Am I patient with teachers new to the profession?
4. How could I reach out and have a positive impact on a teacher?
5. Do I openly gossip about a teacher with other parents?
6. Have I encouraged other parents to become discontent with their child's teacher?
7. When faced with a teacher whose actions I disagree with, do I try to visit with the teacher in a face to face meeting? If no, why not?
8. If my child relates a story where it appears the teacher may have reacted in a less than professional way, do I fact find or assume my child is able to tell the full story?
9. Do I write emails to the teacher when I am angry?

10. Have I forged half truths about a teacher because I felt it is the only way to get rid of the teacher?
11. When a teacher is falsely under attack, do I respond with silence or do I try to defend the teacher?
12. Do I believe my child deserves special treatment in the classroom?
13. Have I completed a random act of kindness for any of my child's teachers?
14. Have I taken the time to compliment a teacher, making sure the administration receives a copy of the email?
15. Have I ever dropped by a teacher's room and confronted him about a problem I perceive?
16. When teachers appear to be unfair, do I question it with the teacher first or do I go straight to the administration?
17. Have I considered becoming a teacher? If no, why not?
18. When I feel the need to correct a teacher, do I address the teacher face to face in a respectful way?
19. Can I contribute to the national conversation to affirm teachers in any way? If so, what might that look like?
20. Do I treat teachers the way I would like to be treated?

Teacher Questions:

1. Do I openly speak negatively about my colleagues?
2. Have I publicly supported my colleagues, even though I may not agree with some of the decisions made in their classroom?
3. Am I patient with my department members?
4. Do I spend time mentoring my department members who may be struggling?
5. Have I allowed staff into my office to complain about a colleague, even though the colleague was not present to defend himself?

6. Do I become defensive when questioned about my teaching practices or am I able to listen to constructive criticism?
7. When faced with a colleague whose actions I disagree with, do I try to visit with the colleague in a face to face meeting?
8. Do I fact find or assume students are able to tell the full story without bias?
9. Do I write emails to my colleagues when I am angry?
10. Have I forged half truths about my department members because I feel that is the only way to get rid of the teacher?
11. When a colleague is under attack, do I defend him? To colleagues? To admin?
12. Do I assume the worst and prone to gossip about my colleagues?
13. Have I completed a random act of kindness for any of my department members?
14. Have I taken the time to compliment a colleague publicly?
15. Have I ever dropped by a colleague's room and confronted them about a problem I perceive? Before class? During class? After class?
16. Do I genuinely love kids, my job and teaching or is this position a stepping stone to something better?
17. Am I able to take the bad with the good? Or will I quit at the first sign of problems?
18. When I do feel the need to correct a colleague, do I address him in a respectful manner?
19. Is there a way I am able to contribute to the national conversation to affirm teachers? If so, what might that look like?

20. Do I treat my colleagues the way I would like to be treated?

Administrator Questions:

1. Do I openly speak negatively about absent staff in admin meetings?
2. Have I publicly supported my staff, even though I may not agree with some of the decisions made in their classroom?
3. Am I patient with teachers?
4. Do I spend time mentoring teachers who may be struggling? If not, is there a mentoring program in place?
5. Have I allowed staff members into my office to complain about a colleague, even though the colleague was not present to defend himself?
6. Have I supported parent complaints at the expense of my staff?
7. When faced with a teacher, whose actions I disagree with, do I try to visit with the teacher in a face to face meeting?
8. Do I fact find a complaint or assume students (or colleagues, parents) are able to tell the full story without bias?
9. Do I write emails to the teacher when I am angry?
10. Have I forged half truths about a teacher because I feel that is the only way to get rid of the teacher?
11. When a teacher is falsely under attack, do I defend the teacher?
12. Do I believe if the child said it (and the parent complained about it), therefore it is true?
13. Have I completed a random act of kindness for any of my staff?

14. Have I taken the time to compliment a teacher publicly? If I do publicly praise my staff members, am I mindful to insure all staff receive equal recognition?
15. Do I drop by teachers' rooms and confront them about a problem I perceive? Send vague emails demanding a meeting? Schedule confrontational agendas three days or more in advance so the teacher worries about the situation?
16. When teachers appear to be unfair, do I automatically assume the worst?
17. When I was a teacher, what were the successful traits of my administrator?
18. When I do feel the need to correct a teacher, do I address the teacher (face to face meeting) in a respectful way?
19. Is there a way I am able to contribute to the national conversation to affirm teachers? If so, what might that look like?
20. Do I treat teachers the way I would like to be treated?

CHAPTER 12: NEW VOICE, NEW MOUNTAIN

Retirement or Permanent Vacation? I didn't lose my job. I succumbed to the fate of politics and age. Three hundred and fifty-seven days have elapsed, and retirement seems just as baffling now as then. Do I regiment my days or remove any reminder of deadlines? Retirement possesses the capability of breeding discontent, depression and a lack of relevance. All three continue to haunt me.

Since the fall of 1971, teaching dictated my life's journey. Granted, transition months intermittently appeared, but even those times filled up with teaching in my voice studio. Bustling down highways, I felt anxious about on time arrival. People who traveled the speed limit upset my plan for expedient travel. Didn't their work assignment demand faster acceleration? For 46 years, I fantasized cruising a back road, driving with the windows down, with no rush and no stress. Now I long for those previously regulated days. Sam Hunt captured me in one of his songs: "doing 15 in a 30, I'm taking it slow just as fast as I can."

Over four decades, the minute school concluded, I embraced vacation mode. Sleeping in without an alarm presented itself as pure luxury. My morning consisted of reading the paper, sipping my coffee and watching The Today Show, HGTV or Fox News. The afternoons and evenings continued free from confines. I deserved a break and took one willingly.

After two weeks into the vacation period, the walls closed in on me. My life appeared without direction, income or regiment. So I began my summer ritual by starting up my voice studio for additional revenue and working on next year's choir plans. Thus the summer would run its course.

Not of my choosing, May 25, 2017 presented itself as the capstone of my career. The summer of 2017 began as most. For the first time in my adult life, a permanent break pervaded my existence. I held tightly to the days without a timetable. Two months into this so-called retirement vacation, I experienced discontentment and depression. When I could function, I updated my resume and joined local and state job sites. No positions found for a retired music teacher. Interestingly, my teacher job skills did not translate into the business world. Fighting mental, emotional and spiritual turmoil, my life seemed without purpose or hope. Most mornings upon awakening, I relived my dismissal, word for word. When it developed into the elephant in the room, I knew the bell tolled for me to arise from bed and attempt the human ritual of living productively or at least, getting dressed.

The fall passed with futile job searches. Thankfully my voice studio and retirement pay sustained me both monetarily and emotionally. A "pity party for Paula" wove itself throughout my daily mindset. I tried to put it all behind me but it became challenging to rectify how 46 years in this profession abruptly came to an end. The elephant in the room took up permanent residence.

One incredibly bright light presented itself quite by surprise. My son and his family moved within 50 minutes of us after spending the past 12 years hundreds of miles apart. Joyfully, the role of grandma lightened the burden of carrying such a heavy heart. The holidays consumed me with dinners, grandkids overnight, traveling guests and a party like atmosphere.

After the New Year, I vowed to go to the gym and convert the idle time to more productive outcomes. My physical and mental health needed attention. Could I lead a full life after teaching for most of it? Filled with sadness, frustration and emptiness, the epiphany: successful retirement depends solely on grit, fulfilling some purpose and accepting the challenges of the new norm.

My voice students generate real happiness in my soul. Just yesterday, after assessing a new student's voice, the young girl broke down in tears at the news that the maturity of her voice, along with her well trained ears, proved exemplary. She then embraced her mother, who also presented the same emotional response. The scene confused me. Why the tears regarding the young singer's talent? She shared the choir director never encouraged her so the assumption persisted she possessed insufficient talent. Little did she comprehend that day how witnessing her joy filled the void in my soul.

What detoured my life from permanent vacation to a meaningful retirement? The death of my dear friend Charles, to whom this book is dedicated. The paradox of his passing? In my own funeral plans, I formally requested Charles to organize the celebratory music. Instead I composed his eulogy, which culminated in a much-needed therapy for my own life. Charles looked to me for direction during his life. Upon his death, I received light on my darkened path, a result of my inadvertently losing my bearings.

After I returned home from the funeral, I sensed Charles' voice exhorting me to start on my book. A few days later, I began to write, and kept it up ever since. The joy of sharing my experiences lifts my soul. This healing, although not complete, offers me a new perspective: unfair things do happen, and how we respond ultimately determines our peace. Nothing new or riveting in that sentence. A tumultuous journey may cloud and postpone the ultimate destination of restorative health. Welcome the turbulent pilgrimage as it affords immense insight to understanding the human dynamics of enduring pain.

The 4:41 Forgiveness Plan: The most productive way to heal is to forgive. At 4:41 am, 19 months after my dismissal, I found myself wide awake. I sat up in bed, looked at my out of use alarm clock and decided it was time to forgive all those who attempted to wrong me. I wish the moment filled with trumpets, beams from heaven and the sweet singing of angels. It was not. As the saying goes: hating those people is similar to preparing a glass of poison for each to take, only I am the one drinking it. Consumed with animosity for those who did me ill only postponed the healing. While no heavenly orchestrated angel choir performed, I firmly testify my soul overflowed with peace for the first time in over a year. Peace which had not found its way until I became the willing participant to forgive. Do not misunderstand forgiveness as easy or a sign of weakness. Forgiveness is one of the most powerful emotions you will ever experience. It takes time and tremendous effort to move forward. I do experience moments of reminiscing about those colleagues, parents and administrators who went out of their way to rain down hurt. But the difference now is that I put a stop to the pain by simply stating, "4:41 Forgiveness is still intact."

Pursue Pause: Setting aside quiet time and reflecting on good things proves restorative in nature. After many years of labor-intensive teaching, contemplating life in stillness challenges me. God cultivated a plan for my life from the very beginning. He used people, both in a negative and positive way, to lighten, darken and detour my path. My odyssey entrenched itself in the day to day rigors of teaching. God actually gifted me a life detour through the actions of a few determined to remove me. Writing a book postponed itself each summer. Time now walks alongside me as my friend.

Through months of developing a manuscript, I truly understand the incredible things which happened to me. In the tranquility of writing, decades of memorable teaching highlights flowed from the back recesses of my mind. The following five examples, although challenging to limit, represent the very best moments of my career:

1. A parent stopped by our sing-a-round at the elementary school where I taught. Through a lump in her throat and watering eyes, she confided her husband left her that morning. She brought her two little girls to school with the intension she would go home and end her life. When she heard our singing, she knew it wasn't the right choice for her and her family. Her sharing the impact music made on her life decision helped me understand the power and medicinal attributes of music.

2. A junior high school girl casually stopped by while I awaited my students' arrival for class. I didn't know her but she claimed I saved her life! Her friend, a singer in our choir, confided in me several days previous she was worried since the girl in question, suffering from depression, appeared absent from school. I summoned the counselor, who called the girl's mother at work. Her mother came home and interrupted the girl from committing suicide. I knew the real answer. God breathes wisdom to those who are willing to listen and whispers compelling words for immediate action.

3. My choirs' selection three years in a row to sing for the state's Holocaust Commemoration ceremony provided the highlight of my career. I researched Hebrew and Yiddish music. One of our young men, a rabbinical student, worked with the choir every day to insure integrity in both languages. On the third year of our performance invitation, the release of *Schindler's List* provided a backdrop to our study. With

parental permission, I invited the choir to my house to view the movie. The bonding that evening traveled far beyond my expectations. The movie's music enriched the film with authentic Hebrew and Yiddish songs. When I found a choral arrangement medley from the movie, assuredly I must teach it. The event took place over 25 years ago yet I remember it as yesterday. On the evening of the commemoration, the statehouse filled to capacity. Candles lit in the darkness and the air resonated with solemnity. Midway through our choir's first song, I heard weeping behind me. The emotions of those in attendance paralleled my students. The poignant connection to the performance, expressed by those young singers, demonstrated music's ability to connect young and old alike. The Holocaust cataclysmic horrors softened, if even for a moment, in the atmosphere of songs of its people performed by students who genuinely reflected the love for all humanity.

Featured as the speaker for the event, Elie Wiesel (1928-2016), a well known author and university professor, presented a soulful eulogy. When we finished performing and people quietly left the venue, this winner of the Nobel Peace Prize took the time to invite my singers to Boston University to study with him. He conveyed adulation for the choir's learning of the Hebrew and the Yiddish with integrity and emotion. I shall never forget the radiance in Dr. Wiesel's face as he complimented the singers.

I sensed a small in stature lady, probably in her 80s, waiting for Dr. Wiesel to finish visiting with us. As she approached our singers with an unsteady walk, tears welled up in her eyes. With a voice determined to speak, the husky sound of the older woman barely presented an audible whisper. She inquired if we knew why so many quietly cried during the first song. The question followed by silence. The woman, herself a Holocaust survivor, spoke in quiet earnestness to the choir encircled around her: this lullaby, first sung by Jewish mothers to their infants, embodied the sweetest yet darkest moments in a mother's life. In the death camps, this song pervaded the hearts of mothers mourning the loss of their children. The power of music to move people proved more evident on that single evening than any other time in my life.

4. I took three choirs to our state's gala event honoring the state's top-rated choirs. We performed Eric Whitacre's *Sleep*. It is an incredibly difficult a cappella piece, written from six to eight separate parts. The chords are dissonant, with voices singing independently. One of my choirs heard a university choral ensemble perform this challenging song the previous year. Students requested me to order the piece, so reluctantly I did. The lower range of the basses went well beyond high school. The intricacy of the parts presented challenges unlike any previous piece. As I expressed doubt, the students stood determine in our performing the piece. Thankfully, the basses could sing below the bass clef and the choir maintained the solidity of the often formidable chordal structure. Combining all three choirs presented a huge risk as finding time outside of school to rehearse created logistic and transportation issues. As the choirs filled the stage of the university performance hall, trepidation filled my heart. By the end of the first phrase, I sensed something surreal. The audience sat in absolute stillness, seldom experienced in today's culture. Their hearts beat with ours. As the piece progressed, the sound elicited proved beyond anyone's expectations, including mine. It didn't happen often for a reason. Finding 90 high school singers to commit themselves to a single outcome proves, by its very numbers, almost impossible. Tremendous perseverance by the singers, to connect with each other at one moment in time, demonstrated

a musical journey like no other. When the last unison note fell into nothingness, the audience, not wishing to interrupt the moment, spent several seconds in silence. Then they stood at once and gave us an ovation like none I've ever experienced. At the intermission, other choirs waited outside for us and physically shook hands and hugged my students.

When I returned home that evening, I sought out parents who attended the concert to see if anyone videoed this breathtaking event. To my disappointment, no videoing permitted due to the constraints of the hall. The following day, I addressed my singers with the sadness we would never playback that incredible musical moment. As the class groaned in unison, Casey raised his hand emphatically. With the wisdom of a sage, he reminded us if the recording existed, eventually we would find fault with parts of it. With no recording, we could give ourselves permission to conjure up the performance without the interference of critiquing it. Just yesterday, I met a former student for coffee. When I asked her if she performed as a part of the *Sleep* concert, her instant smile and exuberance validated she shared the stage that evening. Both of us walked through the rehearsal preparation, laughed at the hardship of finding rehearsal time and ultimately reminisced about a phenomenal concert as we sipped coffee in the warm, mountain sunshine. Neither of us shared any fault in the performance. Casey's idea worked!

5. Success, defined by fame and monetary worth, proves counterproductive if not dangerous. Many of today's young people truly believe the deception they possess the skills which will elevate them to star status. I tread lightly when sharing the stories of my former students, who actually achieved fame in the performance industry: James Valentine plays guitar for *Maroon 5*; Scott MacIntyre sang his way to the top eight in *American Idol*; his brother Todd performed in a

national Broadway tour; Scotty Johnson plays guitar with the *Gin Blossoms* and Nate Zuercher performs with *Judah and the Lion*. Their success is a cautionary tale. Whereas all possess extreme talent, they experienced some good karma and pure luck to be at the right place at the right time. The proper people crossed their paths and mentored them, helping each one to achieve influence and prosperity. I do not take any credit for their success. Seeing them pass through my orbit mandated I keep a vigilant watch to affirm all my singers, as they could be the next ones discovered. I reminded my eager students, while these young men maintain high visibility with a national audience, many performers exist who exhibit success in their own right, but not lucky enough to enter the national stage.

The young man who made Top 8 in *American Idol* invited me to attend the live Top 10 show. Within two days I drained my savings, purchased an airline ticket and made a hotel reservation. Upon arriving, I discovered my trip from the hotel to the studio needed immediate attention. The hotel hailed me a cab and told the Russian driver I needed to go to the CBS studios. A language misunderstanding took me to the CVS Pharmacy! The 15 minute ride turned into an hour and a half of trying to convince this Russian the exact location of the CBS studios. I arrived just as the doors started to close. Witnessing Scott performing on national television made the horrific travel in the open air cab worth the while. I will never forget that magical evening. The most amazing point of all this? My former student is blind. It was an incredible experience watching him navigate the stage, using the microphone as he played his own accompaniment on the piano.

Teachable Moment: Be true to yourself and bloom where you are planted. Take one day at a time, commit to your talent, perform in any venue and maintain the passion. Fame, fortune and the national stage do not guarantee happiness. Making music for the sake of your soul will provide the authentic, inward satisfaction to a life well lived.

Two Cents Worth with Change Back: Embrace teaching but make sure you do it for the right reasons. You must possess a heart for children. Some questions you should contemplate:

1. Do children intrigue you?
2. Do they make you laugh?
3. Do you find a real joy in watching them learn?
4. Do you want to make a difference?
5. How do you feel about working for less pay than your peers in the business world?
6. Do you possess tough skin, enough to sort through unreasonable requests and criticism?

When I started in 1971, I fell sorely short of the above considerations. Only through God's grace did I find my delight in teaching. Here is some free advice: if the only reason you want to teach is because nothing else holds your interest, please rethink your decision. If you want to teach as a stepping stone to a better job, again please reconsider. If you approach teaching in this light, that suicidal student, the culturally deprived children, the child who acts out because of abuse will never receive the necessary attention from you. Our children deserve educators who demonstrate a genuine investment. In a culture which appears void of human empathy and civil discourse, skilled teachers become the bridge between the naive child and the astute adult.

The Legend of the Horse: Rabbi Shraga Simmons tells the story of a farmer who owned a horse: One day the farmer's horse ran away. All the people in the town came to console him because of the loss. "Oh, I don't know," said the farmer, "maybe it's a bad thing and maybe it's not."A few days later, the horse returned to the farm accompanied by 20 other horses. (Apparently he had found some wild horses and made friends!) All the townspeople came to congratulate him: "Now you have a stable full of horses!" "Oh, I don't know," said the farmer, "maybe it's a good thing and maybe it's not."A few days later, the farmer's son was out riding one of the new horses. The horse got wild and threw him off, breaking the son's leg. So all the people in town came to console the farmer because of the accident. "Oh, I don't know," said the farmer, "maybe it's a bad thing and maybe it's not." A few days later, the government declared war and instituted a draft of all able-bodied young men. They came to the town and carted off 100's of young men, except for the farmer's son who had a broken leg. "Now I know," said the farmer, "that it was a good thing my horse ran away."

When I heard this story for the first time, it imbued my soul. I understood why God allowed me to experience wonderful, sad and appalling episodes throughout my career. My forced retirement motivated me to record my thoughts on paper. Contemplating these past 16 months, I now understand God's new purpose for my life. Battered teachers, who are too afraid to come forward, need a voice. Will my rocky experiences deter prospective teachers away from the classroom? They must not. In 46 years, only two fall seasons did I dread to return to the classroom. That dread evolved from the caustic adults in residence and never the children. The minute I walked into my classroom, filled with fun loving kids who wanted to learn, my yearly decision to return proved validated. A career adorned with accolades, admiring parents and supporting administrators would produce a dull read.

Welcome the crises of life and evoke the words of Henry Kissinger: *a diamond is a chunk of coal that did well under pressure.* Celebrate those days which feel like weeks. Affirm the criticism as a path for growth. My narrative has a great ending. After 46 years of teaching, knowing what I know now, I would not change anything!

Teachable Moment: I can now link the dots of disappointment. In 1987 my parents disinherited me. Some of the most rewarding days of my career occurred the years after. When my financial comfort zone diminished in 1987, reality forced me to see teaching as a lifelong pursuit, not merely a stepping stone to something better. Putting into context the obstacles and the sometimes madness of teaching takes months and even years. Or in my case, a lifetime.

Method to My Madness: A movie scene depicted a teacher attempting to run off copies for the day's lessons. The copier, determined not to cooperate, created a line of impatient staff members. The teacher ventured all the usual tricks to persuade the copier to work: opened a multitude of doors, wiggled trays, and gave the usual thump to the machine itself. The teacher began sweating and hyperventilating, showing signs of a nervous breakdown. His colleagues rolled their eyes, offering no support. And then he erupted! Grabbing the paper and drawers of the machine, he slung them through the air. The teachers waiting in line ducking for cover. As expletives spilled forth, he tore the machine a part. He finally encountered the massive ink cartridge. Yanking it out, he opened it and sprayed it all over the room, in machine gun fashion, taking particular aim at his colleagues. This hyperbolic episode played out comedically for the benefit of movie goers. However those of you who rely on copy machines will certainly attest to the volatility of that contraption and the angst it could create.

What is the relationship of this scene with writing a book? In sharing my experiences, I realize teaching seems a bit mad. Movies depict teachers anywhere from buffoons to heroic super humans. Somewhere in-between lies the truth. Be assured those hectic, mad days will be followed by more reasonable ones. Do not let the bumps in the road become permanent road blocks. The tears of frustration are replaced with tears of joy when a student demonstrates true understanding of a concept or he publicly proclaims you made a difference. Sometimes those special God-given moments happened a couple times a week. Occasionally, they occurred hour by hour. One of those divinely inspired moments occurred when Andrea spoke.

Andrea's Voice: The room, dimly lit, appeared quite small for the assigned meeting place. A round table, placed in the center of this cramped space, accommodated eight chairs. Sleet pummeled the window as we waited for more to join us. It appeared the inclement weather affected the turn out. Small snippets of conversation could be heard. Two women, visiting quietly about their experiences, while three others began introductions. I waited nervously, wondering what impact this meeting might have on my life. Women, demoted and demoralized as teachers, gathered to share their story. Most transferred out of the district. Two bowed to the fate of involuntary retirement. Andrea, the last woman to arrive, patiently listened to the hushed conversations. The teachers' union representative opened the meeting and asked the assembled women to introduce themselves and share their experiences. As each teacher spoke, the accounts became more grueling in context and breadth.

All of us, mostly over the age of 40, experienced bullying behavior from our administrators. The effort exerted by those admin teams forced all of us into leaving our positions. In most situations, the offending administrator was male. How could these career professional women receive evaluations riddled with false accusations, experience harassment and derogatory comments? How could our colleagues and community not demand justice? How could years of evaluations with the highest scores of 4 altered in the last year of their employment to 1's and 2's? Modus Operandi (MO): a particular way or method of doing something, especially one that is characteristic or well-established. Make no mistake. An unambiguous MO intertwined itself throughout all of the narratives. Administrators set forth to rid themselves of older teachers in a very unsettling procedure.

Lacy, a teacher forced to retire, stopped the conversation cold with two words: *Exile Isle.* She received the privileged information from teachers working towards their admin certification. The mentoring principal shared this term at their inservice. A unison gasp emitted with incredulous glances at the sound of those words. A cacophony of questions came from everyone in the room. What was this? How could it exist? How was this even possible?

Exile Isle is a term used to compel teachers into resigning or retiring, thus avoiding the firing process. When teachers quit of their own volition, no recourse exists to litigate damages against the district. My ordeal substantiated the implementation of *Exile Isle* as the end game designed for me. Tenure, with excellent evaluations, should have insured my sustainability in my position. The *Exile Isle* procedure appeared multifaceted and scripted by administrators:

- Early in the fall term, veiled verbal and emailed accusations cast a shadow on integrity.
- The administrator sided with any complaining parents, making no efforts to fact find.

- Emails with vague agendas periodically requested meetings with an administrator. Meetings always scheduled in the middle of the day so returning to classes, after receiving a verbal rough up, presented its usual challenges.
- Three to four confrontational meetings per semester, behind closed doors without witnesses, proved debilitating.
- Answers to questions raised, regarding supposed classroom scenarios, never garnered even a nod of affirmation from the administrator.
- Each additional meeting, administrators became more direct with printed out, unfounded accusations. The questions from previous meetings, already asked and answered, reappeared.
- The tone of the meetings began to take on a demeaning nature by midyear. "This meeting is for you to listen and for me to talk" stated by one administrator.
- No rational answer would satisfy the administrator's growing distrust.
- At the EOY evaluation, teachers could return but in a lesser position. This MO prevailed throughout the evening of discussions.

On my daily drive to school, instead of experiencing the incredible beauty of the area, I found myself praying for strength and wisdom. No supplication could alleviate the knot in my stomach wondering if today would produce one of those "gotcha" meetings. The target painted on my back as the admin team went out of their way to make my life miserable. *Exile Isle* was not a familiar term at the time. Reexamining my final year, my banishment to *Exile Isle* began in the fall of 2016, which ultimately resulted being kicked off the island permanently in the spring of 2017.

Receiving a text of an ongoing ice storm during the second hour of the meeting, I apologized for the need to leave immediately. Lacy indicated Andrea needed to share her story. The reality that two hours elapsed with our opining embarrassed me to quickly find my chair. Andrea observed in dedicated silence. Unfortunately, wrapped in our own grief, we forgot to encourage her to speak.

Andrea, in her late 30's, deliberated on our accounts, gazing earnestly with her hazel eyes. She shown forth a most satisfying countenance, willing herself attentive so others could feel heard. I asked Andrea to share her story, secretly ashamed my thoughtlessness in not asking why she attended the meeting.

Andrea taught social studies. She spoke with convincing passion about loving "her kids" and wanting to achieve as the best teacher possible. For the first time in the evening, all sub-conversations ceased. Through her unassuming comportment, she powerfully spoke of her fate.

Andrea shared her best and worst moment, for they breathed the same air. She taught a unit on the Viet Nam war, implementing additional learning tools to broaden the view of her students. Mesmerized by the content of the lesson, the students demonstrated their willingness to initiate their own additional research. Andrea received emails from parents. Not the dreaded negative sort but instead complimentary to her approach in the classroom. Parents reveled in their delight that their children used computers for research instead of playing games. Andrea beamed with pride at her students' eagerness to go beyond the expectations. Her eyes misted as she continued her story.

The day after the unit concluded, Andrea received an email from her principal requesting a meeting. This same administrator followed the *Exile Isle* plan previous to this summons, questioning and admonishing her on a regular basis. Her voice faltered as she fought back tears.

Hoping for a turning point in her relationship with the administrator, Andrea held out that perhaps he finally wanted to pat her on the back for a job well done. With so many parents emailing their support for her and the students demonstrating a real excitement for learning, why couldn't this meeting reveal itself as pleasant?

The principal invited her into the office and closed the door behind her. No one else attended. Andrea began to experience an ominous vibe. No kudos delivered today. She tentatively sat down as the principal began to question her about her unit of study. Andrea was raised with the same naiveté as I. Experiencing genuine success, how could anyone cast a pall of disapproval? And yet, they did. Alluding to the positive emails, Andrea made one last stab at turning the conversation into a positive. The principal scolded her for adding additional curriculum, with an emphasis she could never add on to the plans again. This followed by the threat that if she continued down this road, she might not have a position next year. Sound familiar? Her heart sank. Everything she loved about teaching demolished that day by the Common Core idiom and the masterfully scripted scolding by the principal. How could she tell her adoring students their research, creativity and going the extra mile made for her Achilles Heel? Andrea did something many of us would find challenging. She stayed for the remainder of the year, if nothing else for "her kids."

Andreas exist everywhere in our district, city, state, region and country. No pretense resides within her passion, dedication and iron will. She loved teaching and dreamed of becoming a teacher, even as a child. Where is she now? Andrea, like so many, quit this noble profession. My heart ached for her. Later in the evening, I shared her plight with a friend. As I neared the end of her story, I spoke through a lump in my own throat. I no longer wanted retribution for my poor treatment. I wanted justice for Andrea and all those like her. She cannot speak up for herself, due to her age and employment status. I challenge all to take up her fight and start affecting change today. Talented teachers, like Andrea, should not have to endure menacing administrators, who feel compelled to isolate their unwanted staff to *Exile Isle*. I found my advocacy voice and now I encourage others to commit to that same cause.

The Still Small Voice Within: I dedicated this book to a dear friend, Charles Bowling. He and I collaborated for 10 years providing show choir camps for children grades 3-12. It was an incredible experience that only now, I am fully able to appreciate. As Paul Harvey used to say, "And now the rest of the story."

In the fall of 2012, my high school students asked to celebrate African-American music through the study and performance of spirituals, gospel and soul. No hesitation existed. There was no other African-American teacher with the talent to accomplish this other than Charles Bowling. When he and I did similar clinics in the past, we always ended with "He Never Failed Me Yet" which included student improvisational solos. My heart knew it was time to contact Charles and conduct our favorite song together. I flew back to my homes state, set up a meeting with Charles and eagerly anticipated visiting with my friend and colleague.

It was late January of 2013 when Charles met me at the local coffee shop. I heard him call my name but I could not see the man. Finally, in the far corner, I saw this frail figure who did not appear to have the energy to rise and greet me. I knew Charles was grappling with illness but his demeanor shocked me. The once fierce, fiery singer and choral conductor was a mere shadow of himself.

We visited enthusiastically about the project but I could see the energy drain in his face. Charles was on board and ready for the challenge of working with over 100 of my singers, in spite the telling signs of exhaustion. We jointly picked the music and parted with a quick hug, one which spared his vulnerable frame.

Upon arriving back to the mountains, I kept questioning whether this dear man capable of traveling a long distance, withstanding the high altitude and working on his feet for hours at a time. God nudged me to give Charles a way out in case this assignment presented too many complications. We visited on the phone and in that conversation, Charles gallantly stated he just didn't think his health could withstand the travel and physical demands. I certainly understood and felt a small bit of relief. That would be one of the last times Charles and I talked.

In December of 2017, Charles called and left a voice mail. He seemed upbeat and full of love. He wished my husband and me a wonderful holiday and affirmed he loved us both. After a pause, he said there was no need to call him back. So I didn't. Less than 30 days later, I would hear of his death from his sister. Not taking the time to return his call still haunts me. If only....

This morning, 397 days after Charles' passing, I felt God's love more vibrant than I experienced in years or perhaps ever. My heart filled with so much joy I became overwhelmed with tears and a strong sense of divine affection. Skeptics would label the moment as heartburn or arterial fibrillation. Perhaps

Charles asked God to collaborate with him to reach out to my soul. Brother Charles could persuade anyone to accomplish the impossible! The still voice within swelled with the knowledge that God allowed me to experience 46 years on the thrill ride called teaching. His servant Charles, were he still on earth, would be cheering me on to complete this manuscript, 22 months in the making.

New Voices: Teachers no longer need to cower in their classrooms because of the adverse mental and emotional environment. *Students* receive the first nod to initiate the conversation for change. The "me first" mindset proves itself one of the downfalls of a self-centered society. Why do I never get a break from my teachers? When will the spot light shine on me? Why does life prove itself so unfair? In the first 20 years of my career, only once did parents come to school demanding I justify my teaching practices. All those years ago, students privately vented to their family. Parents then encouraged their children, through role modeling, to work harder rather than complain. They understood their children emulated imperfection. Treating teachers with respect prevailed as the norm. The "me first" child cannot change their mindset without modeling from their parents. Empathy for the teaching profession beacons as a trait desperately needed.

Parents receive the next nod to launch a dialogue of transformation. Our 21st century culture proves fast paced and sometimes void of quality family time. Parents find themselves in a mad rush to procure the most and best of everything for their children. Finding a quick fix for their unhappy child "oppressed" by his teachers steals the focus. Encouraging a child to do better is now cast in the shadows of "it's the teacher's fault" mentality. The general lack of respect for teachers should not surprise anyone. It began in the late

90's when the internet made fast communication possible. Instead of taking time to assess the situation or fact find, parents assume their child incapable of wrong-doing, then reactively write a mean-spirited email and hit send.

Take a moment and contemplate all of the positive influences your children's teachers contribute to you and your family. Go to that computer, in your pajamas if necessary, and email your child's teachers how much you appreciate them! Become a part of the school's parent group, not to criticize but to affirm. Do not be tempted to play the adversary. If you become upset with something your child shared about his teacher, never assume your innocent child brought home the complete story. Research the actual evidence before you blame. Ask questions instead of defending statements of half-truths. If you cannot physically approach the teacher and hold a thoughtful conversation about issues, do not hide behind your computer. Marching straight to the administration proves counterintuitive to speaking with the teacher first. You face four choices: forget the indiscretion if it proves itself something unimportant to the overall scenario; forgive the indiscretion if not purposeful in nature; ask for a face to face meeting with the teacher to ascertain the facts, not confront; after speaking with the teacher and you feel unheard, then finally comes the time to involve the administration. This fourth and final choice should only be used if you deem the situation serious. Serious as defined by the child ceasing to learn, becoming school-phobic, and/or unethical behavior of the instructor.

A *community* conversation must be initiated on the effectiveness of the local school board. Does the school board reflect the expectations of their constituents? Do taxes reflect a positive, meticulous use of funding or are they used to pay off litigations brought forth by unfairly fired or demoted teachers? Does the board demonstrate an awareness of problems in the district? Does the school board actually hold power to effect change? Does the superintendent come across as approachable or does he play the role of politician? As one of my banker friends thoughtfully stated years ago: children are our highest ranked asset, whose rate of return grows over the lifetime of the parent. Shouldn't school boards take an active role in children's schooling in order to receive the highest rate of return?

Teachers need to step up and take a proactive stance. National strikes and contract conversations are in their infancy and hopefully will give birth to a national movement. This past year, teachers went on strike for better pay and benefits in three states. The disparity of pay proves itself only one facet of the discussion. Teachers commit themselves as career educators, never believing at the end of the day they will attain great wealth. The very least teachers should expect in their professional day to day encounters? A work place without fear of harassment, bullying or disrespect from parents, students or their administrators. Perhaps the new mantra for teachers gathers its collective breath from the movie where the man shrieked: "I'm mad as hell and I won't take it anymore!"

The final heart-to-heart exchange is facilitated by staff and their *administration*. One person's claim of being mistreated will not receive serious attention. Ten to twenty teachers, meeting with their administration, could result in change. I reflect back on the annual three to five teachers in any of my assignments who were made to feel inept and unwanted. We, as a staff, missed an opportunity to stand up for them and demand the administration cease its dissenting tactic of persecuting those teachers. One administrator questioned, regarding his inability to protect his staff, replied,

"I kept quiet because I needed the job." That lack of character can no longer persist. If arbitration warrants itself, do so immediately rather than letting the issue fester. Assuring children's best interests should be the litmus test of every conversation. As a battered *Exile Isle* member, my days in the classroom did not prove as effective when I needed to recover from a hostile administration's mid-day meeting. Five parent complaints garnered my dismissal. The shortsighted administration did not take into consideration the 145 parents who supported what transpired in my classroom.

Making a Difference: I loved teaching. With its idiosyncrasies, colleague drama, parental complaints, and work load, those adverse elements canceled by the knowledge teachers do influence lives and help direct students' paths to success. Consider your own educational experiences: the teacher who genuinely cared when you botched an assignment; the field trip where an abundance of planning initiated before one child left the school grounds; the amazing conversations with a teacher who valued your opinions; the creative activities planned in order to make you aware of your world; the sadness on a teacher's face when someone appeared bullied or hurt; the tears occasionally shed in class for the emotionally charged music or subject matter. Students formulate their opinions, ideas and courage to express themselves in a classroom learning environment created by a teacher. Students touch teachers' lives as well. My own self worth thrived when students articulated unbiased ideas, exhibited growth in their skills and supported one another in the classroom.

Important factors for the successful educator include passion, pedagogical knowledge, communication skills and an assertive disposition. While some of these attributes may need honing, no alternative exists for passion. I began my pilgrimage as naive, unskilled and reticent to commit. Twelve years into this profession, I finally grasped teaching a lifetime career. Do not endure 12 years in any profession without understanding your true purpose. Be conscious in your commitment, assert yourself to develop the best teaching practices, and approach each day with fervor.

The platitude of "putting kids first" weaves itself through most curriculum discussions. Let's make sure the slogan does not appear as a clever caption on a school district's website. The future of this country lies in the next generation as they journey through their first 12-13 years of public school education. Putting them first translates into paying teachers a salary which needs no further supplemented income, insuring teachers have a supportive environment to make a difference in a child's life, and shielding them from ignorant, biased attacks.

It is never too late to better our schools, affirm our career teachers, or encourage new teachers. As these excited new teachers join our ranks, we must commit ourselves and pave the way to retain those teachers. Why would any district go to the work of holding job interviews, finding the best candidates and then make those new hires glaringly aware they chose the wrong profession? I experienced incredible jubilation when employed in 1971. New educators should illicit that same delight. This profession held high esteem in our culture forty-six years ago. We need to invigorate yesteryear's support of this noble profession.

New Mountains: My favorite quote comes from Robert Schuller (1926-2015), a well known evangelical pastor. I printed it on a bedrock, which stood guard in my classroom for years. Here is the (paraphrase): "When faced with a mountain, I will not quit. I will either go around the mountain, tunnel through it or climb over it. Better yet, I will stay and turn the mountain into a gold mine." The mountain personified teaching where I remained dedicated 46 years, and the precious gold mine symbolic of the 6000 students whose lives intertwined with mine.

I subscribe to daily, positive thoughts from Joel Osteen, another well known evangelist. The following, from Pastor Osteen, best reflects my new aspiration: *In the Bible, Caleb helped lead the people of Israel into their Promised Land. But Caleb didn't just stop there. In fact, when he was 80 years old he said, "God, give me another mountain." He was saying, "God, give me something else to do. Give me another assignment." Notice, he was planning on living out his life in victory. He could have said, "God, just let me retire. Medicare wouldn't pay for that latest prescription. I'm so aggravated." No, he was strong. He was energetic; he was ready for the next challenge.*

No matter how old or how young you are, God has another assignment for you. You wouldn't be here if God didn't have a purpose for you. Make plans for another victory!

I am a Teacher: That is to say I was a teacher until I was summarily dismissed, fired, forced to retire on April 25, 2017. I am not sure which term fits my demise best. Now I know in part, but shall have a deeper understanding as the years progress, no one may deny me the title of Teacher by actions or words. My smoldering embers of teaching continue to reignite by the advocacy bonfire burning brightly for the dignity of my colleagues. God, give me another mountain so I may rescue my colleagues from believing they hold no importance. God, give me another mountain so I may help save a child.